The Spirit of Project Management

This book is dedicated to all those who have a responsibility for programmes or projects and who are seeking a higher purpose to their work, who are exploring their spirituality, and are developing their higher consciousness in every aspect of their life including their work.

The Spirit of Project Management

JUDI NEAL
and
ALAN HARPHAM

GOWER

Published by
Gower Publishing Limited
Wey Court East
Union Road
Farnham
Surrey, GU9 7PT
England

Gower Publishing Company
Suite 420
101 Cherry Street
Burlington
VT 05401-4405
USA

www.gowerpublishing.com

Judi Neal and Alan Harpham have asserted their moral right under the Copyright, Designs and Patents Act, 1988, to be identified as the authors of this work.

British Library Cataloguing in Publication Data
Neal, Judi.
  The spirit of project management. -- (Advances in project management)
  1. Project management. 2. Spirituality.
  I. Title II. Series III. Harpham, Alan.
  658.4'04-dc23

Library of Congress Cataloging-in-Publication Data
Neal, Judi.
  The spirit of project management / by Judi Neal and Alan Harpham.
    p. cm.
  Includes bibliographical references and index.
  ISBN 978-1-4094-0959-5 (hbk) -- ISBN 978-1-4094-0960-1 (ebk)
  1. Project management. 2. Spirituality. I. Harpham,
  Alan. II. Title.
  HD69.P75N43 2011
  658.4'04--dc23

2011052223

ISBN 978-1-4094-0959-5 (pbk)
ISBN 978-1-4094-0960-1 (ebk)

MIX
Paper from
responsible sources
FSC® C018575
www.fsc.org
FSC

Printed and bound in Great Britain by the
MPG Books Group, UK

CONTENTS

LIST OF FIGURES

LIST OF TABLES

PREFACE

While the topic of spirituality and project management may not seem all that personal, and may in fact seem downright strange to some, it has been an important part of our personal and professional journeys. Perhaps it has been an important part of yours as well, although you may not have had the language to describe it. We hope that this book opens your eyes, heart, and mind to notice the ways in which spirituality may already exist in your project managing, and that it inspires you to take further steps to expand purpose, meaning, and inspiration in the work you do.

Alan started his life as a civil engineer. A number of things about such a career appealed to him in his youth. Firstly, he had an uncle who he only saw from time to time when he came back from his latest foreign overseas project. These projects were usually based in exotic, far-flung parts of the world. As he listened to his uncle's travel stories, Alan loved the idea that such a career would bring lots of traveling and experience of fascinating places, stories and religions. His uncle also brought back many exotic and exciting gifts, things seldom seen at home in the UK.

As he grew older, Alan read some of the materials about a career in project management. He read that civil engineers took nature and put it to work for the betterment of humankind and that sounded like a wonderfully fulfilling and purposeful career. He saw himself as managing nature rather than working with it. Many define "spiritual" as that which gives meaning and purpose in life (Fairholm 1997,

Mitroff and Denton 1999) and this felt like a career that would be deeply spiritual – not that Alan was thinking that way as a young man.

Later, after many years as a civil engineer, he felt less good about project management work when he looked at mankind's efforts in the world and all the threats humankind was potentially facing. He began to think that these threats were possibly because of mankind's very use of nature and its exploitation. As an old Native American said of White people:

> *The White people never cared for land or deer or bear. When we Indians kill meat we eat it all up. When we dig roots we make little holes. When we build houses, we make little holes. When we burn grass for grasshoppers, we don't ruin things. We shake down acorns and pine nuts. We don't chop down the trees, kill everything. The tree says, "Don't. I am sore, don't hurt me." But they chop it down and cut it up. The spirit of the land hates them. They blast out trees and stir it up to its depths. They saw up the trees. That hurts them. The Indians never hurt anything, but the White people destroy all. They blast rocks and scatter them on the ground. The rock says, "Don't. You are hurting me." But the White people pay no attention. When the Indians use rocks, they take little round ones for their cooking ... How can the spirit of the earth like the White man? ... Everywhere the White man has touched it, it is sore. (McLuhan 1992)*

Since he was a civil engineer he has had three more careers: the first as a University lecturer in the School of Management at the University of Cranfield where he began to satisfy one of his highest values – the growth and development of others (and indeed himself). He was director there of one of the world's first MSc's in project management. Four years later he became a management consultant focused on transforming the way organisations managed their investment for strategic change and its portfolio of programs and projects. He did this for 16 years with Mike Nichols, Chairman of the APM, and loved every assignment and training course. Many of the latter were held in the outdoors to help people with their interpersonal skills, similar to how

Joseph Jaworski (1997) describes it in his book *Synchronicity*. Alan is now part-time chairman of an Accreditation and Certification body, the APM Group, and also chairman and member of some organisations focused on the spirit at work phenomenon. He is at a very happy stage in his life and by rights should retire!

In parallel with his work he was invited to a meeting at Lambeth Palace crypt to see if a charity called CORAT had any life left in it as its members felt that they were past their sell by date. From that came MODEM, an ecumenical charity interested in encouraging dialogue between people interested in Theology, Spirituality and Ministry, and those interested in Leadership, Organisation and Management. As initial chairman, Alan ensured they look from work to church at first, and they produced a number of books and ran many lectures. After five years Alan stood down as chair and helped to start up a work group to look at from Church to work. This led him to connect initially with many other Christian organisations such as CABE, Chrism, ICF, and many others, as well as organisations for all faiths and none such as The Center for Spirit at Work at the University of New Haven, led by Dr Judi Neal. They became great friends and Alan became a director of the Center for Spirit at Work and also joined the judging committee for the International Spirit at Work Awards. He was also a steward of the Spirit in Business organisation managed between the US and Europe until it ceased. He became friends with the European Bahai Business Forum and many other organisations interested in this topic. Through the Center he also met Cindy Wigglesworth and discovered her pioneering work in SQ – Spiritual Intelligence; Richard Barrett, founder of the Values Center; and Father Thomas Keating from the Magic Monastery in Snowmass. Judi Neal has left the University of New Haven and is now Director of the Tyson Center for Faith and Spirituality in the Workplace at the Sam M. Walton College of Business, University of Arkansas.

When Darren Dalcher asked Alan if he would write a book on *The Spirit of Project Management* he laid down one condition and that was that his co-author would be Dr Judi Neal. Fortunately she accepted the challenge and brought all her expertise to bear.

Judi has been interested in spirituality in the workplace since the early 1990s when she began conducting research on this phenomenon as a management professor at the University of New Haven. Prior to her academic career, which began in 1988, Judi worked in the corporate world in the field of organisational development. While in the corporate world, her interest in spirituality was a private and quiet matter, and seemingly had little to do with her working life.

However, in 1987, Judi discovered that the organisation that she was working for was breaking the law and putting people's lives in danger. She became a whistle blower, and her own life became in danger. That crisis led her to the understanding that spirituality, and a trust in something greater than ourselves, is at the core of life, and cannot be treated peripherally, if life is to have meaning and purpose. She left the corporate world to teach in the Business School at the University of New Haven with a commitment to doing what she could to help future leaders to be more values-centered and more willing to act with integrity than the leaders she had experienced in her corporate work.

Judi discovered that there were other people in the world crazy enough to want to think about integrating their spirituality and their work, and she became passionate about finding them and creating a community of academics, leaders, and change agents doing this work. That led to the creation of the Center for Spirit at Work, which received international attention for their work on identifying and studying organisations that nurture the human spirit.

The organisation began having an annual conference, and Judi, who had no background in project management, learned by her bootstraps how to be a project manager. Fortunately, she had people like Alan Harpham and Elisa Mallis on her team, who provided wonderful project management expertise. While the projects that Judi works on are not construction projects or projects that send a human being to the moon, her projects do focus on expanding the field of faith and spirituality in the workplace through awards, conferences, research events, and other ways of collectively bringing people together to make a difference. In 2009, Judi was invited to become director of the Tyson Center for Faith and Spirituality in the Workplace at the University of Arkansas, and moved there the same year. She has re-started the International Spirit at Work Awards under its new title, the International Faith and Spirit at Work Awards, and Alan has become part of the awards committee again.

It has been as if there was a very long rope that had project management at the one end and spirituality at the other end. Alan picked up the project management end and followed it towards spirituality, and Judi picked up the spirituality end and followed it to project management.

We, Alan and Judi, met in the middle of that very long rope, and this book is a result of our exploration of the intersection of spirituality and project management. We sincerely hope that you find both inspiration and practical guidance from what we offer here.

ACKNOWLEDGEMENTS

JUDI NEAL

First of all, I would like to thank all of the people over the years who have been involved with the Association for Spirit at Work, which was later called the International Center for Spirit at Work. So many of you were involved directly in our projects and outreach, and you taught me so much about the true meaning of spirituality and project management. I am grateful to the Tyson Family Foundation and the Walton Family Foundation for providing an endowment to set up the Tyson Center for Faith and Spirituality in the Workplace where I could continue to reach out, and connect, to people working in this field. The Tyson Center for Faith and Spirituality in the Workplace has also provided me the opportunity to think more deeply about the role of faith and spirituality in organisations and to explore specific applications, such as to project management.

I wish to acknowledge Alan Harpham, my co-author, for his friendship, support, and encouragement over all of these years and for his trust and generosity in inviting me to join him in this book-writing project. I also wish to acknowledge our editors, Darren Dalcher and Jonathan Norman, for having the insight and courage to support such a non-traditional project management book. Their guidance and feedback contributed to this book in very significant ways.

Daryl Conner and Mel Toomey have been leading experts in the field of leading and managing change, and they both have been extremely encouraging and helpful during the writing of this book. They have seen for a long time the powerful link between spirituality and project management, and they are exemplars of people who walk the talk. Their guidance and wisdom have become so much a part of my thinking and action that I can no longer delineate where their work stops and mine begins.

I also want to thank the members of the Management, Spirituality and Religion (MSR) Interest Group at the Academy of Management, whose work has inspired me and whose friendship has encouraged me. I am especially grateful to Dorianne Cotter, who read an early version of this manuscript and who provided valuable feedback.

Finally, I wish to express my heartfelt gratitude to my husband Ralph Ellis and my sister Marie Wolny who have spent countless hours reviewing the manuscript and suggesting improvements, and cheering me on. Their love means the world to me.

ALAN HARPHAM

I would like to thank all those who have been friends, advisors and mentors during my life.

I am very grateful to John Laings, for my early formation in construction projects in buildings, motorways, pipelines, North Sea oil rig platforms and finally international petro-chem construction projects. Through this I was privileged to visit many countries and cultures. I learnt so much initially working with much more experienced contractors. I remember Dick Storr, an early General Foreman who had worked for Holloways (later taken over by John Laing) in the Middle East in the 1950s. They went on a bachelor status contract for 50 weeks each year with two week's holiday at home. I remember his advice not to follow that path as he did when he did not get to begin to know his son until the son was over 6 year's old – he had seen him for 6 x 2 weeks in that period and felt he never caught up the relationship.

Sir John (the founder of John Laing) applied his values strictly in his business. I first met him as a young boy in the Church Crusaders when he would come and talk about his particularly robust form of Christianity. When I joined the company as an indentured graduate civil engineer a few years later, in the mid-1960s, smoking was not allowed anywhere in head office. Sir John applied his values to his work and all 25,000 employees. While we thought him too paternalistic in those days, one can but admire his wisdom now. Alcohol on expenses was also definitely not allowed while he was at the helm! This became a problem when I worked in JVs with the French on pipelines, and later on the North Sea rigs, as they were definitely into fine wines on expenses. I am grateful to them too for all they taught me!

I would certainly like to thank the Cranfield School of Management for all they taught me on my MBA, and my fellow students from whom I learnt as much, and then as a lecturer later in my career. The late Peter Forrester, who was the first Head of School and was there when I arrived as a student, became a mentor who started my journey into the idea of spirituality at work when, as a leader of CORAT, he invited me as a member of the next generation to see if there was anything worth saving. Here I met the lovely Raymond Clark, a trustee of CORAT (Christian Organization for Research & Training), who helped lead the formation of MODEM, which I became chair of at its launch, an organisation focused on authentic dialogue between those interested in Leadership, Organization and Management, and those interested in Theology, Spirituality and Ministry. As you will know, a modem translates between two systems speaking different languages, and this MODEM recognised the need for communication between spiritual (churchy) language and secular language in business. MODEM and its board members led me to many other Christians and organisations for those with a faith and those with none, such as Judi's Spirit at Work organisation at New Haven. I am grateful to all those who were on the MODEM committee that I led and those who have maintained it since.

In my role as a Christian I have been a church warden, a co-chair of a deanery synod, and a member of a Diocesan Synod. I was also asked to chair the Ministerial Training Scheme (MTS) for the Diocese of St

Albans, where I learnt a great deal from the various principals and staff that I worked with, as well as from the board members (mainly clerics). When MTS ceased and became the St Albans & Oxford Ministry Course I co-chaired it with Bishop Anthony Russell, recently retired as the bishop of Ely in the UK. I was also a volunteer in the assisted self-appraisal scheme for clergy and learned a lot from those whom I assisted.

This, together with my work with Judi's Center for Spirit at Work, is where my interest in spirituality in the workplace developed and I was delighted to encourage two people who have become great friends, David Welbourn and Sue Howard, to write their book on *The Spirit at Work Phenomenon*. I also encouraged David and another friend, Father Dermot Tredget OSB, to found the Spirituality in the Workplace group that has met at Douai Abbey, a Benedictine monastery, for the last 10 plus years. I am most grateful to them and the many members of all faiths, and none, who have taught me so much.

Most recently I became the chair of Workplace Ministry Hertfordshire and Bedfordshire, leading a group of chaplains, some paid, some volunteers working in organisations in the public and private sectors. We have become a charity limited by guarantee, EPI (Ecumenical Partnerships Limited) and are continuing with traditional chaplaincy, putting chaplains into many diverse organisations to get alongside people where they are, to listen to them, to support them and encourage them to be all that they can be in body, mind and spirit. I myself am chaplain to our local ambulance service and am eternally grateful for all they do and have taught me.

I would particularly like to thank some authors who are also friends: Georgeanne Lamont and her book *The Spirited Business*. Georgeanne has also provided some serious training in the organisation I chair – The APM Group – on eight ancient wisdoms (mostly deeply spiritual); and Richard Barrett for his *Liberating the Corporate Soul*, and his sequels and his enthusiasm and drive.

Finally I would like to thank my mentor – Reverend Dr Norman Todd, who I have known since we were together on the board of MODEM in the 1990s and who is still mentoring me now when well into his nineties and with a mind as sharp as a razor. He has led me to writers and books I would never have found without him, and his post-modern ideas on Christ and Christianity are always enlivening.

This is not to forget my wife of more than 40 years. She was a physiotherapy student when I met her at a church in North London where her Uncle was church warden and my father had been the other before he retired to Cornwall. Subsequently, after we married and had two lovely boys, now lovely men, she became a counselor, before becoming an Anglican priest. She is my best friend and my best support. She looks after my body, mind and spirit along with a huge group of other people who look to her for spiritual leadership and support – thank you Di.

Reviews for *The Spirit of Project Management*

Spirituality is a sense of meaning, purpose and wanting to make a difference. Projects are also about making a difference. Judi and Alan have brought together a wide range of sources to put Spirituality into context and provide ideas for greater understanding of oneself and your team. A very thought provoking read.

Richard Pharro, CEO of the APM Group

This book makes a strong case for project management and spirituality being a powerful context for full self expression in the workplace. Judi and Alan's words bring life to the notion that people at work are committed to contributing and making a difference. They do a brilliant job of integrating, what at first may seem, disparate subjects.'

Mel Toomey, D.H.L., Scholar in Residence at The Graduate Institute, Bethany, USA

Of great interest to anyone concerned with (or about) Project "Humankind." The combination of wide experience of project management, and open explorative spirituality with a vision of future development, is a call for responsible study and action. I hope that others will be encouraged to explore the emerging spirituality in their own "secular" work and share it as lucidly and creatively as these authors. I also hope that all spiritual and religious traditions will recognise their own roots in such emergence and set about examining their management of their own God-given project.

The Revd Dr Norman Todd, former Adviser for Bishops' Ministry
to the Archbishops of Canterbury and York

Read this book for a vision of wholeness. Judi and Alan hold together what we so often seem mad keen on dividing – a sense of the spirit, and competence in getting things done. They show with wit and humanity that you can live a life of spiritual wisdom without losing the plot. Great!

The Rt Revd Paul Bayes, Anglican Bishop of Hertford

Spirituality in our everyday lives – not just on Friday, Saturday or Sunday – is truly our best hope for a peaceful world. This important book shows how everyone involved in projects and programmes – from the CEO to the newest team member – can work in harmony with their spiritual lives. Obviously our projects must align with our organisations' strategies, and our daily work on them must also align with our spiritual aspirations.

Russell D. Archibald, Honorary Fellow APM/IPMA, PMI Fellow, PMP
and author of *Managing High-Technology Programs and Projects*

Alan and Judi expose a critical consequence for spirituality in project management: enhancement of the collective spirit of the team, the recipient of its created value, and in turn, the organisation itself. Too often, project management has been considered only a technical discipline, yet by its very nature, project management is a social discipline that can only be enhanced by bringing a renewed sensitivity to spirituality in the workplace. In a world rapidly becoming overcrowded and overstressed, a focus on spirituality is not an option, nor is reading this book. They are both imperatives for every project manager.

Gregory Balestrero,Retired President and CEO,
Project Management Institute

The authors bring together the generally structured world of project management with the often diffuse area of spirituality. By comparing different approaches at levels from the personal to the planetary, they raise important questions about where similarities and differences exist, and where mutual learning between different disciplines can take place.

Tim Harle, Visiting Fellow, Faculty of Business and Law, University of the
South of England, Lay Canon, Bristol Cathedral and Vice-Chair, MODEM

'In writing this book the authors remind us of the long-forgotten and vital spiritual component of business life, and how to get a better balance into our management methods – one that will bring greater success. In giving practical advice, through examples as well as tools and techniques, they help many of us do what we know we should be doing already. They propose an exciting new future, one where the full potential of people and teams is realised – probably the only way we can deal with the complexity of the modern world.'

John Kay, Director of Change Management, Transforming
Business and former partner at PA Consulting Group

THE CONTEXT FOR SPIRITUALITY AND PROJECT MANAGEMENT

The book is divided into two parts: one which provides background material and one which provides practical application material. In Part I, we provide a context for spirituality and project management. We take a look at the background of project management by exploring the history of the field and making the case that spirituality has always been interwoven into the work of project management, although it has seldom been explicit. We then take a look at the history of spirituality in the workplace as an emerging field.

CHAPTER 1

BACKGROUND OF PROJECT MANAGEMENT IN A SPIRITUAL CONTEXT

In this chapter, we look at projects in history and their connection to religious and/or spiritual purposes. Project management has ancient and sacred roots, and it is our hope that this book will help to re-inspire the connection between spirituality and project management.

Let's start at the beginning of civilisation. In the early days of project management it would seem most major projects were created for a spiritual purpose. This was often based on a belief in an afterlife and the need to go into this next life in the best possible condition. These projects were funded by extremely wealthy rulers, emperors, and kings, who literally owned everything in their lands – the land, the natural resources, and the people (Figure 1.1).

Earliest among these projects are the ancient pyramids of Egypt[1] and South America,[2] circa 2000BC, built to such high standards that we still do not know how they were achieved! Huge blocks of stone were cut and laid in such a way that it is impossible to insert a piece of paper between them. What was their purpose? Today we are beginning to know something of the power of pyramids to preserve meat kept in its center of gravity where the embalmed bodies of the Pharaohs were laid to rest, often surrounded by riches to use in the next life.

---

1   The earliest among these is the Pyramid of Djoser (constructed 2630 BCE–2611 BCE).
2   The start of the pyramid building era in Mesoamerica dates back to between 1800 BCE–200 CE.

Figure 1.1   Early major projects

Sources: Hagia Sofia © Uozdil | Dreamstime.com; Terracotta Warriors © Contax66 | Dreamstime.com; Rumkale © Hayk Harutyunyan | Dreamstime.com; Great Umayyad © Angela Ostafichuk | Dreamstime.com; Mayan Pyramid © Joao Virissimo | Dreamstime.com; Gisa Pyramid © Francisco Caravana | Dreamstime.com

Preserving life to go on to the next life was of utmost importance, whatever that next life might have been.

Then, at Xian in China, we have the extraordinary discovery of the Emperor's huge burial site,[3] of which only a fraction has so far been excavated. Acres of land covering a whole army of terracotta warriors and then a circus and other entertainers, a zoo, and a menagerie of terracotta and bronze animals have been discovered, not to mention all the chariots and other transportation, all ready for this one man and his afterlife.

This was a dangerous time and place to be the Project Manager as the emperor usually insisted that all those who knew their way into the tombs, and the treasure stored there, should be killed at the end of the construction phase of the project. So the Project Managers took all their secrets to the grave with them, leaving no possibility of the secrets being sold or traded.

Then later, the earliest civilisations building in Syria near the Euphrates had fresh running water and sewerage systems working around five centuries BC. The Euphrates is thought by many to be the setting for the Garden of Eden.

Damascus, Syria, is the world's oldest continuously inhabited city in the world. In its midst is the Great Mosque, originally built as a Greco-Roman temple to Zeus in 64 CE, converted to a Christian basilica dedicated by Constantine to John the Baptist in 391, becoming a mosque in 634 CE. Inside is a shrine to John the Baptist venerated by both Christians and Muslims, and it is the fourth holiest place in Islam.

Later, from 500 BCE to 400 CE, we have examples of first the Greeks and then the Romans building extremely fine buildings to meet and live in, as well as some magnificent temples. Their ruins can still be

---

3   Work started on the site in 246 BCE when Qin Shi Huang, later the first Emperor of all China, ascended the throne.

seen today in countries around the Mediterranean and were once the envy of many other parts of the world.

Christianity became a force in the world around 2,000 years ago. The Roman Emperor Constantine began a magnificent church project in Constantinople (now Istanbul), a huge church named the Hagia Sophia or Divine Wisdom (circa 360 AD). Constantine originally built a much smaller church, and it was Justinian who built the present building, in 532 CE, after the previous basilica burnt down. This too, like many churches, was later converted to a mosque and is now a museum. From the time of the Prophet Mohammed onwards, Islam erected beautiful buildings to worship and honor Allah and these too have stood the test of time, as well as inspiring their builders and visitors.

Many beautiful churches and cathedrals were built from stone throughout Europe (circa 1100–1700 AD) with many artisans being employed in their construction. These are buildings that were built to last and continue to attract visitors and worshippers from all over the world.

More recently (circa 1700s), the Shah Jahan built the magnificent tomb for his wife, Mumtaz Mahal, in white marble inlaid with gemstones, the Taj Mahal. His original plan was to build a black mirror image building for his own tomb on the opposite bank of the river and then link the two with a suspension bridge made of pure silver. In the event, before he could do this, his son took him captive and murdered his own brothers in order to inherit the kingdom. This prevented the further construction, but left one of the Seven Wonders of the World with its many visitors to admire her tomb. It is worth adding that rather than put the architects to death, Jahan offered them all land to own and settle on so that they would not go off and build anything similar for another emperor – their descendants still live around Agra to this day.

The people who built the buildings were clearly inspired in their work. The purpose of many of the buildings was to reach for the transcendent and to help the people who used the buildings to do the same. Many buildings were used to worship a God or higher power and glorious images were used to assist in that process.

As human beings evolved and developed over the ages and as their consciousness has expanded, so too has the nature of projects, moving on from construction into science and engineering projects and, more recently, into IT, communications, aerospace, pharmaceuticals and energy. Project Managers of modern day projects are still seeking the same kind of esprit de corps in their project teams, high innovation and creativity and inspirational leadership, as existed in these earlier projects. They are looking for that feeling that comes from creating something much bigger and greater than one's self, and for the benefit of others.

Mankind has always felt the pull to create with others inspiring and lasting projects to honor the transcendent and the self. If spirituality is truly that which gives meaning and purpose in life then it seems very obvious that work is a major provider of spirituality and that projects within work, those one-off events, have the capacity to provide many with real meaning and purpose in their work.

Projects, like human beings, also have lifecycles. Humans are born, grow and develop, become productive and re-produce, wane, slow down, and ultimately die. They start with a lot of uncertainty and head for the only certainty in life – their death. Projects start as a germ of an idea, become a concept, are defined, designed and firmed up. They are then manufactured or created for real, being put to use or sold, until eventually they reach the end of their lifecycle and are killed off, taken down or perhaps apart, or simply fall down to be overtaken by the next idea or project.

Projects are run and delivered usually by project teams and these go through stages too. The most commonly known are group development states of forming, norming, storming, performing, and finally adjourning (Tuckman 2001) when the team completes the project and parts company into the individuals who go off to new projects and new teams. Many find this cycle of creation ending and starting again very invigorating for a fulsome life – some find the ending very sad.

In the 1960s we saw the advent of space projects. Yuri Gagarin, in 1961, was the first cosmonaut from Russia and then we saw the American race to put a man on the moon in 1969 – the Apollo space project. While not originally initiated as a spiritual project, it has been fascinating to see how many of the Apollo Astronauts, once they have seen their home from outer space, the friendly, pretty little blue planet – earth – have become very interested in their spiritual side.

Edgar Mitchell was so in awe of looking back at earth from space that he experienced a spiritual transcendence that was to define his life's work. He founded the Institute of Noetic Sciences, which seeks to take a scientific approach to understanding human consciousness and the experience of transcendence. Indeed, we understand that the first thing that Neil Armstrong did after landing was to seek a little time out to share a communion wafer he had taken with him, just before opening the door and making that "one small step for man, one giant leap for mankind."

It is not often that one hears the words "spirituality" and "project management" uttered in the same sentence, and yet this review of the history of project management from our earliest times points to a much stronger connection between the two than one might first imagine. We believe that spirituality is an inherent part of any project, just as spirituality is an inherent part of any human being.

In this chapter we have looked at how the purpose of many ancient projects, as well as many down the ages, including today, have met a religious or spiritual need.

In the next chapter, we will explore the newly emerging concept of spirituality in the workplace, which lays the groundwork for our particular application of spirituality to the field of project management.

CHAPTER 2

BACKGROUND ON FAITH AND SPIRITUALITY IN THE WORKPLACE

In this chapter, we provide a brief history of the faith and spirituality in the workplace movement and define some of the more common terms used, such as spirit, spirituality, faith, and religion. Three models for the development of human consciousness will be briefly presented, and guidelines for discussing spirituality in the workplace will be provided.

HISTORY OF THE SPIRITUALITY IN THE WORKPLACE MOVEMENT

Just as spirituality has been an integral part of project management since the earliest times of civilisation, it has also been central to work and to organisational systems. As humans formed families and families formed tribes, one of the important roles in each group was the shaman, priest, or healer. These were the people who were in direct touch with the world of the gods. Their role was to find direction from the gods for the good of the tribe, and to intercede with the gods on behalf of tribal members. They performed ceremonies and rituals. They prayed. They blessed the hunt. They healed the sick.

Today, it is not uncommon to have a priest or pastor provide a blessing for the breaking of ground of a new building. In Asia, some organisations bring in a feng shui practitioner to provide guidance on building layout, design, and furniture placement for the best use of spiritual energy. Many business leaders rely on prayer and spiritual guidance for difficult business decisions or new business challenges. For example, when Indra Nooyi accepted her position as Chairman and CEO of PepsiCo, her first official act before flying to corporate headquarters was to go to her Hindu Temple to pray. Michael Stephen (2002), former Chairman of Aetna International, attributes his success in entering the insurance markets in China and Latin America to his spiritual practice of Transcendental Meditation and his daily attendance at mass.

While spirituality in the workplace has been with us for millennia, as a field of study it is very new. The earliest book that was explicit about the value of integrating spiritual values in the workplace was by Robert Greenleaf, entitled *Servant Leadership* (1977). After that, there was very little, if anything, in the literature until the early 1990s. Since that time there has been a dramatic increase in the number of books, conferences, journal articles, and newspaper articles on the topic. For a current bibliography, go to the Tyson Center for Faith and Spirituality in the Workplace website and click on "Resources" (see http://tfsw.uark.edu).

DEFINITIONS

Before examining some of the forces that led to this increase in interest, it will be helpful to define and draw distinctions among some of the common terms that are used. For the purposes of this book, we use the term "spirituality" because we believe it is the most inclusive and accessible term. Other words that are often used interchangeably are faith and religion, but we see these terms as related to each other, yet distinct.

The word "spirit" comes from the Latin words "*spirare*," to breathe and "*spiritus*," the breath (Fox 1994). Breath is that life force that enlivens and sustains us. Christians speak of the Holy Spirit as the breath of life, and when someone dies we say they "gave up the ghost." In other words, their spirit and their breath left them. Hindus practice *pranayama* as a way of integrating greater *prana* or life force. Shamans have a healing practice of breathing energy into a patient through a reed or straw.

"Spirituality" is most commonly defined as connection (Sense and Fernando 2011, Mitroff and Denton 1999). Fairholm defines spirituality as follows:

> *One's spirituality is the essence of who he or she is. It defines the inner self, separate from the body, but including the physical and intellectual self [...] Spirituality also is the quality of being spiritual, of recognizing the intangible, life-affirming force in self and all human beings. It is a state of intimate relationship with the inner self of higher values and morality. It is recognition of the truth of the inner nature of people. (Fairholm 1997: 29)*

The Merriam Webster dictionary provides several meanings for spiritual, including these top three:

1 : of, relating to, consisting of, or affecting the spirit : incorporeal <*spiritual* needs>

2 a : of or relating to sacred matters <*spiritual* songs>
  b : ecclesiastical rather than lay or temporal <*spiritual* authority> <lords *spiritual*>

3 : concerned with religious values

The dictionary definition for faith is similar, but tends to be more focused on religion:

1 a : allegiance to duty or a person : loyalty
  b (1) : fidelity to one's promises (2): sincerity of intentions

2 a (1) : belief and trust in and loyalty to God (2) : belief in the traditional doctrines of a religion
  b (1) : firm belief in something for which there is no proof
  (2) : complete trust

3 : something that is believed especially with strong conviction; *especially* : a system of religious beliefs <the Protestant *faith*>

In common usage, people often define themselves as "spiritual but not religious." In the US, more than 30 per cent of the population fit into this category, with this number growing every year according to a

2009 Newsweek poll. That same poll found, however, that 48 per cent of the US population defines themselves as "religious and spiritual" (Stone 2009).

When we talk about spirituality in the workplace, many people immediately become concerned because they think that this means religion in the workplace. But this is one of many myths. Spirituality in the workplace, and by association, spirituality in project management, does not have anything to do with promoting a particular religion, or in promoting religion in a more general way. Religion is a personal and private choice in free, industrialised nations, and it is important to keep it that way. Another misconception about spirituality is that it is equated with "spiritualism" or mediumship. A third misconception is to equate faith with religion. Most people have faith in something greater than themselves, but they may or may not be a member of a particular religion.

Figure 2.1 depicts the overlapping nature of these three concepts, showing that each one is distinct from the others and yet there are areas of similarity between them.

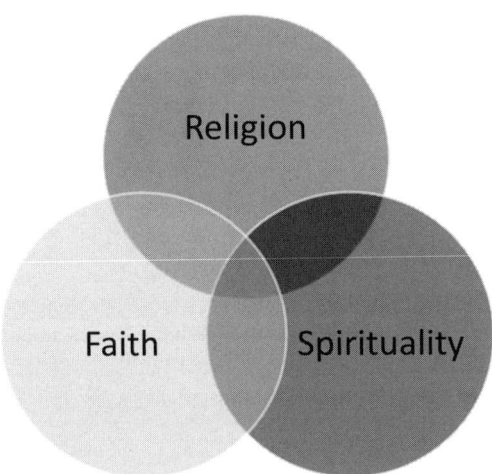

Figure 2.1   Interconnection of religion, faith, and spirituality

From 2001 through 2008, both authors were involved in the International Spirit at Work Awards, a process that identifies organisations that nurture the human spirit, and honors them at an annual conference. It is very helpful to see how spirituality is defined for these awards. The following list of characteristics of spirituality in the workplace (Table 2.1) comes from the International Spirit at Work Award application form and is based on the work of Wilber (2001), who defines spirituality as having both vertical and horizontal components.

Table 2.1　Definition of spirituality in the workplace from the International Spirit at Work Awards application form

• The innate human attribute in spirituality. All people bring this as an integral part of themselves to the workplace. Spirituality is a state or experience that can provide individuals with direction or meaning, or provide feelings of understanding, support, inner wholeness or connectedness. Connectedness can be to themselves, other people, nature, the universe, a god, or some other supernatural power.
• The "vertical" component in spirituality – a desire to transcend the individual ego or personality self. The name you put on the vertical component might be God, Spirit, Universe, Higher Power or something else. There are a great many names for this vertical dimension. This dimension is experienced as a conscious sense of profound connection to the Universe/God/Spirit. This might be experienced internally as moments of awe or peak experiences. A strong, sustained vertical component reflects in outer behaviors as a person (or group) who is centered and able to tap into deep inner strength and wisdom. Generally quiet time, time in nature, or other reflective activities or practices are required to access the "vertical" component of our spirituality. Examples of the vertical component of spirituality might be meditation rooms, time for shared reflection, silence before meetings, ecumenical prayer, and support for employees to take time off for spiritual development.

Table 2.1   Continued

• The "horizontal" component in spirituality – a desire to be of service to other humans and the planet. In the horizontal we seek to make a difference through our actions. This dimension is manifested externally. A person with a strong "vertical connection" who is also able to demonstrate the "horizontal dimension" has a clear grasp on his/her mission, ethics, values. A strong "horizontal" component is demonstrated by a service orientation, compassion, and well-aligned vision/mission and values that are carried out in productive and effective services and products.
• Spirituality in the workplace means that employees find nourishment for *both* the vertical and horizontal dimensions of their spirituality at work. Spirituality in the workplace is about individuals and organisations seeing work as a spiritual path, as an opportunity to grow and to contribute to society in a meaningful way. It is about care, compassion and support of others; about integrity and people being true to themselves and others. It means individuals and organisations attempting to live their values more fully in the work they do. Examples of vertical organisational spirituality include: meditation time at the beginning of meetings, retreat or spiritual training time set aside for employees, appropriate accommodation of employee prayer practices, and openly asking questions to test if company actions are aligned with higher meaning and purpose. Companies with a strong sense of the horizontal will generally demonstrate some or all of the following: caring behaviors among co-workers; a social responsibility orientation; strong service commitments to customers; environmental sensitivity; and a significant volume of community service activities. The vertical and horizontal dimensions should be well integrated – so that motivations (sourced from the vertical) and actions (horizontal manifestations) are explicitly linked. We will be honoring organisations that are financially sound, sustainable, and effective, as well as focused on greater meaning and purpose. We believe that when done properly, Spirit at Work enhances the overall value of the organisation.

TRENDS THAT LED TO INTEREST IN FAITH AND SPIRITUALITY IN THE WORKPLACE

There are three primary trends that have led to the interest in spirituality in the workplace. The first is the changing psychological contract that has occurred in the past 20 years. When Judi Neal was growing up, her father worked for a company called Raytheon; in fact, he worked for that company his whole life. He never expected to work for another organisation. He was a loyal "Raytheon Man." Today, no one expects to work for the same organisation throughout their entire career. In fact, very few people expect to even stay in the same career.

Beginning in the late 1980s, organisations began to change their psychological contract with employees so that they no longer guaranteed a job for life. Mergers and acquisitions became common, and the attendant downsizing led to many people realising that the corporation was no longer going to provide them their identity and security. For many people this was a spiritual crisis. They began to see that a more spiritual approach to life could help them find an inner identity and security that was no longer going to be supplied by the external world.

A second contributing factor to the growing interest in faith and spirituality in the workplace was demographic. The baby boomer generation began to reach middle age in the 1990s, and middle age is often a time of asking oneself deep spiritual questions as we reflect upon the life we have lived so far, and contemplate the second half of our lives. The three great spiritual questions are:

1. Who am I?
2. Why am I here?
3. What am I supposed to be doing?

The third contributing factor was the approaching Millennium. It became a time when humanity collectively began to reflect on the last 2,000 years and to contemplate what the next 2,000 years might bring for the human race and the planet. Collectively, we asked ourselves these spiritual questions:

1. Who are we as a human race?
2. Why are we here?
3. What are we supposed to do to sustain life on the planet?

As a consequence of these three factors, many scholars, leaders, and consultants began to look at the way organisations are structured, the way they are led, and to ask questions about the deeper purpose of business, beyond making a profit for its owners or shareholders. The 47 organisations that received the International Faith and Spirit at Work Award are examples of organisations striving to find a more spiritual and values-driven approach to business (see Appendix A).[1]

Ian Mitroff and Elizabeth Denton conducted a major study of spirituality in the workplace, published in 1999. Among other things, they discovered that there was more agreement than they expected in how people define spirituality in the workplace. Sixty per cent of those polled by Mitroff and Denton believed in the beneficial effects of spirituality in the workplace, so long as there was no promotion of traditional religion. They are currently replicating this study in Europe and their findings are very similar.

Warren Bennis (1999), in the foreword to Mitroff and Denton's *A Spiritual Audit of Corporate America*, says:

> *Individuals and organisations that see themselves as "more spiritual" do better. They are more productive, creative and adaptive. The people in these organisations are more energised and productive because their work isn't solely about stock options and vacations and coffee breaks. Spiritual organisations are animated by meaning, by wholeness, and by seeing their work connected to events and people beyond themselves. (Bennis 1999)*

Handy (1994), an Irish management guru with strong spiritual connections who is considered one of the most influential management thinkers, coined the term "portfolio worker" to describe the change

---

1   For a more thorough discussion of the trends in faith and spirituality in the workplace, see Chapter 2, "The Corporate Interest in Spirituality" in *Religion and the Workplace*, by Douglas Hicks (Cambridge, UK: Cambridge University Press, 2003); and *The Spirit at Work Phenomenon*, by Sue Howard and David Welbourne (London, UK: Azure, 2004).

from "organisational man" to a worker now having jobs for a short period and a number of jobs making up a career. He also said that what people need in life is "meaning and purpose" (often used as a definition of spirituality) and to work in community with others. The project life is one where people come together on projects for one to five years and form a new community, then disband, and then reform, usually elsewhere in a new team, and so on throughout life, very much like Handy's "portfolio worker." What can often be missing is the fulfilment of the need for meaning and purpose, and a sense of community at work.

DEVELOPMENT OF HUMAN CONSCIOUSNESS

The trends described above can be seen as a special case of a more generalised growing consciousness and emotional and spiritual evolution in the human race. There are numerous authors who have different models of the development of human development, from moral development (Piaget 1932, Kohlberg 1981, both of whom influenced the work of Ken Wilber (2001)), to ego development (Cook-Greuter 1990, 1999, Kegan 1982, Loevinger 1976), to faith development (Fowler 1981). Three authors that have specifically focused on spiritual development in a work context are Don Beck (Beck and Cowan 1996), Richard Barrett (2006), and Cindy Wigglesworth (2006, 2010).

What all of these models have in common, according to Spence (2006), is:

• First, each stage of one's development is characterised by a qualitatively different epistemology, affecting the manner by which an individual views reality.

• Second, the stage sequence of development is unidirectional and is similar for all individuals or groups of individuals, and for progression to occur, Rooke and Torbert (1999) note that "… a person or group must master the characteristics of an earlier level before moving to the next one" (1999: 2).

- Third, the sequence is hierarchical toward an increasing integration, where each stage serves as a foundation for all that follow. In becoming increasingly more integrated, Cook-Greuter (1990, 1992, 1999) contends one's self-view becomes less distorted, enabling a closer relationship to objectivity or truth.

Father Thomas Keating, a contemplative monk from the St. Benedict's Monastery (Snowmass), summarises these three stages in this way:

> *The beginning of the spiritual journey is the realisation; not just the information, but real interior conviction that there is a higher power, or God. Or to make it as easy as possible for everybody, that there is an Other; capital O. Second step, to try to become the Other; still a capital O; And ... finally, the realisation that there is no other. You and the other are ONE; always have been, always will be. You just think that you are not. (Keating 2005)*

We will now briefly describe each of these three models and discuss their relevance for project management. If any of these models intrigue you, we encourage you to read the work of these authors and perhaps to consider bringing in a certified practitioner to work with your team.

SPIRAL DYNAMICS

The following diagram provides an overview of Spiral Dynamics, which was based on a synthesis of earlier work on human development. This model is very useful because it not only applies to individuals, but also to project teams and to organisations. According to Beck and Cowan (1996), as we move from the earlier levels of development to the next level of development, we shift from a focus on self to a focus on community at one level, and then from a focus on community to a focus on the individual at the next level. This could have very interesting training and development implications for a project group as they work together over time. As a project leader, you might ask yourself if the project team's energy is more focused on individualism or on collectivism. Neither is good or bad, and each has a place in a team's development.

The chart below (Figure 2.2) starts with the first Spiral Dynamic developmental level of beige at the top of the chart, and describes life conditions at each level of development, and the way the brain and mind cope with each particular life condition.

	LIFE CONDITIONS			BRAIN/MIND COPING CAPACITIES
A	State of nature and biological urges and drives: physical senses dictate the state of being.	BEIGE	N	Instinctive: as natural instincts and reflexes direct; automatic existence.
B	Threatening and full of mysterious powers and spirit beings that must be placated and appeased.	PURPLE	O	Animistic: according to tradition and ritual ways of group: tribal; animistic.
C	Like a jungle where the tough and strong prevail, the weak serve; nature is an adversary to be conquered.	RED	P	Egocentric: asserting self for dominance, conquest and power. Exploitive; egocentric.
D	Controlled by a Higher Power that punishes evil and eventually rewards good works and righteous living.	BLUE	Q	Absolutistic: obediently as higher authority and rules direct; conforming; guilt.
E	Full of resources to develop and opportunities to make things better and bring prosperity.	ORANGE	R	Muitiplistic: pragmatically to achieve results and get ahead; test options; maneuver
F	The habitat wherein humanity can find love and purposes through affiliation and sharing.	GREEN	S	Relativistic; respond to human needs; affiliative; situational; consensual; fluid.
G	A chaotic organism where change is the norm and uncertainty an acceptable state of being.	YELLOW	T	Systemic: functional; integrative; interdependent; existential; flexible; questioning; accepting.
H	A delicately balanced system of interlocking forces in jeopardy at humanity's hands; chaordic.	TURQUOISE	U	Holistic: experiential: transpersonal; collective consciousness; collaborative; interconnected.
I	Too soon to say, but should tend to be I-oriented; controlling, consolidating if the pattern holds.	CORAL	V	Next neurological capacities. The theory is open-ended up to the limits of *Homo sapiens'* brain.

The theory is open-ended, with the possibility of more systems ahead...

Figure 2.2   Spiral Dynamics
Source: Used with permission, Susie Weller (2010).

It is important to understand that as a person, team or system develops through the levels, the earlier stages of development are understood, and integrated. But it is very difficult, if not impossible, to understand the levels that are beyond one's level of development. Beck and Cowan (1996) state that we all have levels of development within us, and that we tend to see the world through one predominant level, based on our life conditions. It is extremely helpful in project teams to have an understanding of your own level in the Spiral, and to have a sense of what the level of the project team as a whole might be.

Please see Appendix B for a list of "Questions for Discernment and Discussion within Each Stage of Spiral Dynamics," from Susie Weller.

SEVEN LEVELS OF CORPORATE CONSCIOUSNESS

Richard Barrett, author of *Building a Values-Driven Organisation* (2006), was working at the World Bank when he felt called to understand the interconnection between spirituality and the workplace. His study led to the creation of his models of individual, group, and corporate consciousness.[2] This model (Figure 2.3) uses Abraham Maslow's (1943) Hierarchy of Needs as its basis for the first four levels, and then expands on the Hindu chakra system for the higher levels.

Barrett has created a whole system of organisational transformation tools that includes a values assessment based on this model that has been used by organisations around the world in very effective ways. The values assessment can be a very useful tool for project teams that are interested in understanding their current level of group consciousness and are looking for ways to develop to a much higher level of capacity and performance.

---

2   Barrett's models of corporate consciousness can be found on his website. You will also find numerous articles and case studies of how this model has been used in teams and organisations. See www.valuescentre.com

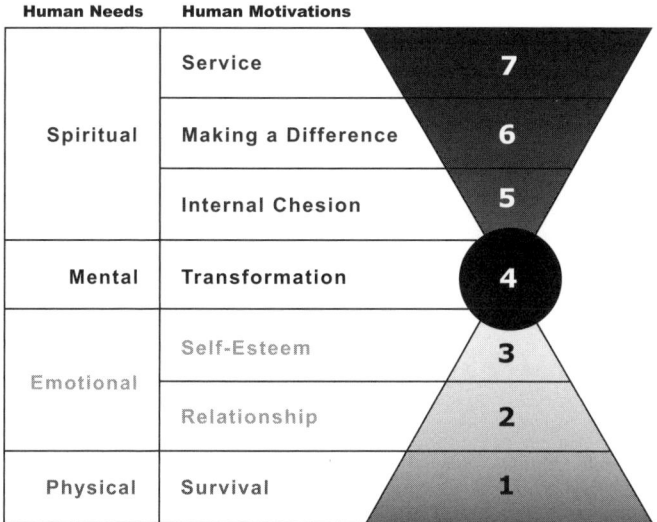

Figure 2.3   Seven levels of corporate consciousness
Source: Used with permission, Richard Barrett.

SPIRITUAL INTELLIGENCE ASSESSMENT

The third model that we believe has great applicability to project teams interested in integrating spirituality into their work is the Spiritual Intelligence work by Cindy Wigglesworth. She defines spiritual intelligence as, "the ability to behave with compassion and wisdom (love) while maintaining inner and outer peace regardless of the circumstances" (Wigglesworth 2006). Goleman's (1994) work demonstrated that emotional intelligence is a better predictor of effective leadership than intellectual intelligence. Wigglesworth has developed a Spiritual Intelligence Assessment model (Figure 2.4) that goes beyond emotional intelligence to incorporate spiritual skills and awareness.

There are 21 factors in spiritual intelligence, and in her assessment tool, Wigglesworth divides these into four quadrants. The quadrants on the left are focused on individual awareness and skills, and the quadrants on the right are focused on the collective, and working with

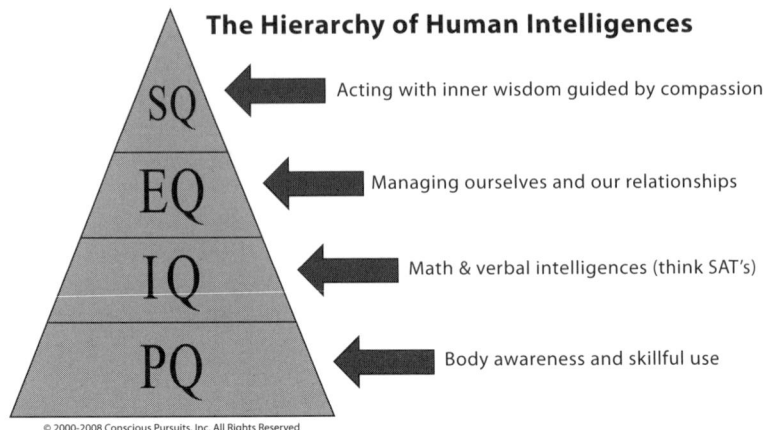

The Hierarchy of Human Intelligences

SQ ← Acting with inner wisdom guided by compassion

EQ ← Managing ourselves and our relationships

IQ ← Math & verbal intelligences (think SAT's)

PQ ← Body awareness and skillful use

Figure 2.4   Wigglesworth's Hierarchy of Human Intelligences
Source: Used by permission, Cindy Wigglesworth.

larger systems. An effective Project Manager, as well as effective team members, need to have awareness and skills at the individual level as well as the more universal and collective level.

The Spiritual Intelligence development process begins with taking the Spiritual Intelligence Assessment (found at www.deepchange.com). Each person receives a report on their level of each of the 21 Spiritual Intelligence Skills (Table 2.2), along with recommendations for how to develop each skill further.

These three models have been widely used in corporate settings and have proven very valuable as tools to help individuals and teams strengthen their spiritual development in the context of work. We invite you to use the grid on page 24 (Table 2.3) to analyse which of these spiritual development models might work in your project team. This will help you to evaluate what you like and don't like about each model and assess how appropriate each one might be for your project team. You can add your own factors, if you wish. Some of the factors listed here might require more outside information, for

Table 2.2   Wigglesworth's 21 Spiritual Intelligence Skills

Spiritual Intelligence (SQ) Skills	
Higher Self/Ego Self-awareness 1. Awareness of own worldview 2. Awareness of life purpose (mission) 3. Awareness of values hierarchy 4. Complexity of inner thought 5. Awareness of Ego Self/Higher Self	**Universal Awareness** 6. Awareness of interconnectedness of all life 7. Awareness of worldviews of others 8. Breadth of time perception 9. Awareness of limitations/power of human perception 10. Awareness of Spiritual laws 11. Experience of transcendent oneness
Higher Self/Ego Self Mastery 12. Commitment to spiritual growth 13. Keeping Higher Self in charge 14. Living your purpose and values 15. Sustaining your faith 16. Seeking guidance from Spirit	**Social Mastery/Spiritual Presence** 17. A wise and effective spiritual teacher/mentor 18. A wise and effective change agent 19. Makes compassionate and wise decisions 20. A calming, healing presence 21. Being aligned with the ebb and flow of life

example learning about the cost comparisons of using each model. Two different ways to rate each factor are:

1. Put a check mark in the box if you have a positive evaluation; or
2. Rate each factor on a scale of 1 to 5 for appropriateness for your team, with 1 being low, and 5 being high.

CREATING ENVIRONMENTS FOR SAFE DISCUSSION ABOUT SPIRITUALITY

It is of the utmost importance to create a safe environment in the project team before beginning any kind of program or approach to integrating greater spirituality. As mentioned earlier, many people confuse terms like spirituality, faith, and religion, and become very concerned that

Table 2.3 Spiritual model evaluation

Model Factor	SPIRAL DYNAMICS	CORPORATE CONSCIOUSNESS	SPIRITUAL INTELLIGENCE
Easy to understand			
Access to expert who could facilitate our work with this model			
Affordability			
A fit with our culture			
Helpful to team members			
Helpful to the team as a whole			

Table 2.4   Flip chart for brainstorming definitions

FAITH	RELIGION	SPIRITUALITY

someone may try to force their religious or spiritual views on them. If this were to happen, it would be very disruptive to the relationships on the project team and to the project itself.

We have found that the best way to begin to create a safe environment is to have a discussion about team members' understanding of spirituality. An easy way to do this is to create three flip charts or a white board with three columns with the words "faith," "religion," and "spirituality." It would look something like Table 2.4.

We ask team members to free-associate or brainstorm words that they feel help define or describe each of these three words. Often there are words that fit into more than one column. As people list words, we write them in the column they request. We may ask for clarification, but it is important not to try to guide or control the conversation. After the list feels complete to everyone, we open up the discussion to ask people what they see as the similarities and differences between these concepts. This feels like a safe way to begin exploring ideas around spirituality, because the definitions have come from the team itself, rather than being imposed by someone else.

After the discussion, we offer the dictionary definitions provided at the beginning of the chapter, and then emphasise that we will not be talking about religion, which is personal and private, but that we are trying to create an environment where people feel safe in talking about what they have faith in, and what feels spiritual and inspirational to them.[3]

In our combined years of experience in the field, we have found the following guidelines very helpful in the beginning of any program concerning spirituality and project management. You may have some guidelines of your own that fit your unique situation and team.

- Spirituality is defined primarily as meaning, purpose, and wanting to make a difference.

- No proselytising or promoting of religion.

- Understand that everyone is a spiritual being.

- Be willing to listen to differences in life experiences and to value and honor them.

- Identify shared values and principles that everyone on the team can agree to.

- Commit to a culture of valuing diversity.

This chapter provided an overview of the newly emerging field of faith and spirituality in the workplace, including a discussion of definitions

---

3   Several PowerPoint presentations that provide introductory material on spirituality in the workplace can be accessed from the Resource section of the website for the Tyson Center for Faith and Spirituality in the Workplace. See http://tfsw.uark.edu

and a description of the trends that have led to the interest in this field. We presented three of the more popular spiritual development tools that could be used by project teams as a way of starting the integration process for greater spiritual awareness and skills in the team, and provided some guidelines for creating safety in project team discussions about spirituality. In the next chapter we will focus on spiritual virtues that are relevant for project teams in a diversity of environments and settings.

CHAPTER 3

THE VIRTUES OF SPIRITUALITY AND PROJECT MANAGEMENT

According to the Hebrew Bible/Old Testament, King David united the 12 tribes of Israel and planned to build a Temple to God. However, God told King David that his son Solomon, not King David, would build the temple. When King David died and Solomon succeeded his father and became King, Solomon prayed for wisdom instead of gold and power. God was pleased at his humility and gave him not only wisdom, but riches and power as well. The leaders of the tribes of Israel had great respect for Solomon and sent him money, materials, and help to build the temple.

It may seem odd to think of King Solomon as a Project Manager, yet building a temple as large and grand as that described in the Bible, was a huge undertaking. His father, King David, had assembled many of the materials over a long period of time, and had begun the design for the Temple, but it was up to King Solomon to actually pull together the manpower and the extra materials to complete the project, one that has been central to Jewish history and all of the Abrahamic faith traditions. It was the finest building in the world at that time, taking 200,000 men a period of seven years to build. It was made of the finest woods, described so beautifully in the Bible. He could not have done this if he had not managed by a set of spiritual virtues.

In this chapter, we suggest that the core virtues of spirituality are essential virtues that need to be at the center of any major project that is undertaken. An interesting paradox exists in this worldview; we believe that the virtues-centered Project Manager will be a highly effective leader, and at the same time, the experience of leading a large and significant project provides the opportunity for one to become more virtues-centered.

THE WISDOM OF SOLOMON

In the book, *Managing with the Wisdom of Solomon* (Manz et al. 2001), the authors draw on the stories of six leaders from the Hebrew Bible to illustrate how business leaders can lead through using timeless virtues. Wisdom is held up as the central virtue because it leads to the other four virtues that the authors feel have the most relevance for modern day leaders:

- The faith of Job.

- The courage of David.

- The compassion of Ruth.

- The integrity and justice of Moses.

There are two kinds of wisdom needed for being an effective Project Manager – practical wisdom and transcendent wisdom:

> *Practical wisdom emerges as a response to the demands of task accomplishment and relating to others. The form of practical wisdom is often tied to a particular place and time: "Early to bed, early to rise, makes a man healthy, wealthy, and wise," "You won't get a good job without a college education," or "Do unto others what you would have them do unto you ... ."*
>
> *Transcendent wisdom is a deep form of knowing that flows from reflection upon experience and is sensitive to the details of human encounters with life. In the Judeo-Christian tradition, this wisdom is closely tied to being faithful to God. That is, the focus is beyond oneself and centered within a broader sense of being. (Manz et al. 2001: 20–21)*

Solomon has asked for "an understanding mind to govern your people; able to discern between good and evil" (I Kings 3: 11–13). It's not difficult to see how that kind of wisdom is essential to business leaders today, and central to the reputation and career of a Project Manager. The Serenity Prayer, attributed to the theologian Reinhold Niebuhr, is one, we are willing to bet, that has been used by thousands of Project Managers in their quest for wisdom in managing change:

The Serenity Prayer

God grant me the serenity to accept the things I cannot change
The courage to change the things I can
And the wisdom to know the difference.

This prayer became popularised through its adoption by Alcoholics Anonymous and is widely known in the mainstream.

In reviewing the stories shared about the biblical characters in their book, Manz et al. conclude:

All of our biblical characters acted on behalf of others with the intent of helping, supporting, building up, or leading. Cultivating wisdom is not an isolated process; wisdom calls us to be mindful of and responsible to the people.

Wisdom becomes incorporated as we seek to develop the spiritual virtues in ourselves and to enact them through our interaction with others and through our leadership. That is, wisdom is fully realized as we encounter each other and build together for the good of all. (Manz et al. 2001: 147)

While the virtues discussed here are found in the stories of the Old Testament, a Project Manager does not need to be Jewish, Christian or Muslim to be informed and inspired by these timeless stories of virtue. In fact he or she need not be religious at all. It is enough to understand that these stories have withstood the test of time and culture, and have something universal to say to humankind.

The virtue of wisdom is also central to Eastern spiritual traditions, such as Zen Buddhism. In *The Zen Approach to Project Management*, George Pitagorsky defines wisdom as:

> ... *applied experiential knowledge – knowledge beyond intellect – based on an unobstructed, unfiltered view of how things are. It is founded on the ability to accept things as they are as a starting point for meaningful, useful action. The ability to accept things as they are is enabled by working from one's "center" – that calm, objective place from which action flows in a way that is perfectly appropriate to the situation at hand ... Everyone can experience a sense of inner peace. Everyone has the ability to take a step back to see things objectively. Doing so makes project success more likely. (Pitagorsky 2007: 16)*

Imagine having this kind of wisdom and inner peace when negotiating deadlines and deliverables with the project stakeholders, or when an unexpected crisis emerges and a cool head is needed to solve problems. Imagine having the wisdom of Solomon when someone brings you an extremely difficult situation and you must judge right from wrong.

DOING VIRTUOUS BUSINESS

"Virtue" is a slightly old-fashioned word in the UK and the US. Perhaps it has seemed too old-fashioned and therefore has fallen out of favor among business leaders, both in dialogue and practice. One exception to this is Wright (2005), who explores the interface between Christian values and the utilitarian and pragmatic consideration of business. He argues that Christianity has turned its back on the business world, and thereby has lost a valuable opportunity to influence the secular world. He believes that religious thinking and business action can come together in worthwhile ways.

There are many lists of virtues, and much research on which virtues are primary, but only a limited number of authors writing about virtues in the workplace. Besides Manz et al., highlighted above, two more of the well-known thinkers about virtues in the workplace are Dr Ted Malloch and Dr Dorothy Marcic.

Malloch is a Research Professor at Yale University and the Chairman of the Spiritual Enterprise Institute. He has been studying spiritual virtues in business for many years and has concluded that virtuous organisations create greater spiritual capital. He writes:

> In referring to spiritual capital I am acknowledging the great amplification of the human spirit that comes through faith. In worship and prayer we entrust ourselves to another and greater power, and we learn to live through trust. In referring our decisions to that higher power we become more confident in making them. And in adopting the discipline and humility that comes from religion we make ourselves ready to account for our failings and to deal honestly with others. (Malloch 2008: 16)

It is not acceptable in the secular world of business to admit publicly that you pray about your decisions. But Jerry Harvey, Professor Emeritus from George Washington University once described to Judi how often CEOs would pull him aside to talk about their faith and spirituality, and to share that they turned to prayer for all their major decisions. None of them were willing to talk about this publicly for fear of what this might do to their image of being rational and data driven, and what it might do to the company's stock price, yet they found prayer and spiritual guidance essential in knowing what to do in challenging circumstances.

While Manz et al. (2001) focus on wisdom as the central virtue, Malloch argues that all the other virtues arise from faith. He says that the fundamental notion of the moral life to ancient philosophers like Plato and Socrates was virtue and that it was not "a matter of what you *do* but what you *are*" (Malloch 2008: 18). His list of virtues is informed by Christian teachings.[1]

For Marcic, the primary virtue is Love:

> *What would it mean if we would love our subordinates, our bosses and our colleagues as ourselves? It would mean we would not intentionally hurt them, we wouldn't treat them unjustly, and we would act towards them with dignity and respect. Such as some of the building blocks of a healthy and thriving system. (Marcic 1997: 15)*

Marcic is a member of the Baha'i faith, and she draws on the seven Baha'i virtues in her discussion about the "New Management Virtues." Table 3.1 shows a comparison of the virtues described by these three authors. This table is not exhaustive, but it provides food for thought for the Project Manager who wishes to clarify the list of virtues that they want to incorporate in their leadership.

We won't go into each of these virtues and its relevance for project management, but we encourage you to define for yourself the key virtues that you as Project Manager would like to strive for. Share your list of virtues with your team, and ask the team to develop a list of virtues to aspire to for the project you are working on.

In this chapter we have focused on the more spiritual term "virtues," but some project teams may prefer to use the word "values" because it is less laden with religious or moral connotations. The Values Assessment process developed by Richard Barrett and mentioned in

---

1   Dr Malloch has created an hour-long video documentary titled "Doing Virtuous Business." It reviews the 14 virtues from his book *Spiritual Enterprise* and provides a corporate example for each, with interviews with CEOs of virtuous organisations. It might be worthwhile viewing for project team members, prior to having a discussion about project team virtues or values. Clips of these interviews can be found at www.doingvirtuousbusiness. com

Table 3.1   Workplace virtues across traditions

Virtue	Manz et.al Old Testament	Malloch Christian	Marcic Baha'i
Wisdom	x		
Faith	x	x	
Courage	x	x	
Compassion	x	x	
Integrity	x		
Justice	x		x
Honesty		x	
Gratitude		x	
Perseverance		x	
Forgiveness		x	
Patience		x	
Humility		x	x
Respect		x	x
Generosity		x	
Chastity		x	
Thrift		x	
Trustworthiness			x
Unity			x
Dignity			x
Service			x

Chapter 2 is an excellent tool for helping teams and organisations examine and realign their values.

Besides all of the virtues described above, some values we have found very useful in project management teams we have worked with include:

• respect for diversity;

• freedom;

- deep listening;

- creativity;

- trustworthiness;

- commitment to something greater than oneself.

We will conclude this chapter with a brief discussion of each of these in the context of project management and include some suggestions for project team activities.

RESPECT FOR DIVERSITY

Wheeler (1996) reports that there are numerous academic studies showing that heterogeneous groups outperform homogeneous groups in problem-solving and creative solutions. Project teams require a diversity of thinking and problem solving approaches. By embracing greater gender, cultural, age, and functional diversity, project teams are more likely to develop multiple perspectives on a problem or opportunity and to select the best solution for moving forward. The spiritual virtue that is core to respecting diversity is actually that of "unity" – of recognising our oneness and our shared humanity.

A mature project team may find it valuable to explore the diversity of a team member's spiritual values, practices, and beliefs, as a way of deepening understanding, respect, and trust levels in the team. Any conversation about something this personal must be handled with the utmost professionalism and the Project Manager must model respect for diversity in this dialogue. This kind of exploration can precede the exercise described above that elicits the spiritual values that can guide the project team in their work and relationship with each other.

FREEDOM

The co-authors of this book have a dream of a world without borders or boundaries, both physical and mental. We need to take down the barriers to thinking that exists on so many projects. Often the need to move on and show some progress means we start without a clear vision of where we are going. If we don't know where we are going, any route will do! Far better to liberate people's thinking at the outset of the project in its conceptual stage and obtain as much creative thinking before freezing the aim and scope to concentrate on the delivery in "short order" time.

DEEP LISTENING

Most leadership development programs teach something about communication, particularly about the importance of listening. They teach active listening skills, and have course participants learn how to feed back to a subordinate or colleague on what they heard the person say. This is extremely valuable, particularly when delegating, and also in more emotionally charged situations such as performance appraisals or performance improvement discussions. Active listening is a very important skill for Project Managers, whether dealing with the project stakeholders, clients, vendors, or team members. But we are talking about something more spiritual here when we talk of the value of "deep listening."

Deep listening is the ability to hear beyond the words and beyond facial expressions. You can only listen deeply if you care about the person and are committed to the project. To listen deeply, you must be willing to trust your intuition, and you must be willing to have an open heart. It is about listening for what *isn't* being said. In order to be effective, you must be willing to share with the other what you think you are sensing in your deep listening. You may not always be right in your intuition, but just the fact that you are attempting to listen at a deeper level will make a difference to the person you are interacting with. It is an example of spiritual connectivity.

As a Project Manager, you can encourage your whole team to value deep listening, and to take the time and energy to listen at this level with each other as well as with non-team members with whom they interact and in particular the stakeholders. One of our former colleagues described it on a railway routing project – putting the people (the public) back into Public Relations. You can also apply deep listening to the project team as a whole, listening beyond the words in a meeting, and beyond the rational and analytical project management processes. It helps to ask what are called "powerful questions" of the team, such as "What's not being said that needs to be said?" or "What wants to emerge here?"

The most powerful kind of deep listening is what could variously be called "listening to the soul of the project," "listening for the still small voice," or "listening for guidance from the Transcendent." Each Project Manager and project team will have their own language for this. A team that is high on spiritual intelligence will acknowledge and tap into spiritual or divine wisdom, particularly at the early stages of the project, and at times when the project experiences roadblocks, breakdown, or crisis.

CREATIVITY

Project management, by its nature, is structured, analytical, process-oriented, and risk-averse. Hillson (2009) and Cleden (2009) distinguish between risk and uncertainty. We like the Voltaire quote, "Uncertainty is uncomfortable; certainty is ridiculous." Hillson and Cleden agree that we live in an increasingly uncertain world, and that one of the main roles of project management is to manage risk. Hillson describes the task of risk management very specifically: "It is to enable individuals, groups and organisations to make *appropriate decisions* in the light of the uncertainties that surround them" (Hillson 2009: 6). He defines risk as "uncertainty that matters" (Hillson 2009: 6).

Cleden states that "for a risk to be identified, we must have a basic level of knowledge concerning the problem" (Cleden 2009: 4). Cleden elaborates that risks can be analysed but uncertainty is an "unknown unknown" and not susceptible to analysis: "It is what is left behind when all the risks have been identified" (Cleden 2009: 4).

It is human nature, when contemplating risk and uncertainties, to adopt a mindset based on fear and problem prevention. This is a useful mindset in some circumstances, but quite limited in its scope. Neal (2006) refers to this mindset as the "Doomsayer" mindset. Fear, when we are attached to it, shuts down the frontal lobe of the brain and lights up the amygdala – the primitive "fight or flight" part of our brains. The temptation in project management is to focus primarily on this fear mindset, which is the opposite of a creativity mindset.

Most spiritual traditions advise us to "Choose love not fear" (Course in Miracles) and to "Fear not" (Christianity). Eastern spiritual traditions see all emotions as ephemeral and much of their spiritual practice is based on noticing the emotion and then letting it go. The inner work of the Project Manager should include some kind of contemplative or meditative practice that increases self-awareness and non-attachment to emotions, particularly to the emotion of fear.

Successful Project Managers cultivate a mindset of openness and curiosity, which is essential for creativity. In contrast to the "Doomsayer" mindset, Neal (2006) calls this the "Edgewalker" mindset. Edgewalkers are leaders who are open to possibilities, curious about what's new and over the horizon, and who are adept at walking the edge between the material world and the spiritual world.

Opportunity management is just as important as risk management, yet very few experts talk about the unexpected and surprising breakthroughs that can happen if one is open to them. We focus on the negative Black Swans, but not on the positive Black Swans. Taleb (2010) popularised the term Black Swan, which he defines as an event with three attributes:

1. *It is an outlier, as it lies outside the realm of regular expectation because nothing in the past can convincingly point to its possibility.*
2. *It carries an extreme impact.*
3. *In spite of its outlier status, human nature makes us concoct explanations for its occurrence after the fact, making it explainable and predictable.* (Taleb 2010: xxii)

In 2011, protests for democracy in Egypt caused Hosni Mubarak to step down from the Presidency, and the accelerating democratic movement swept the generally autocratic regimes of the Middle East. This is an example of a positive Black Swan, something that no one could have predicted, but an event that is now full of creative possibilities for someone open, curious, and creative enough to explore them.

TRUSTWORTHINESS

Trust is the key variable in all relationships according to Gibb (1978). It begins with self-trust, trusting our own instincts and sense of things, as well as trusting our own intentions. He says that without trust in interpersonal, group, or organisational systems, you cannot have productivity and effectiveness. Instead you spend tremendous amounts of time and energy on creating control systems because you don't trust people. A survey of employees by the Chartered Management Institute in the United Kingdom (Miller 2011) found that the attribute most sought after by the staff of their manager was authenticity. Authenticity creates trust.

In your role as Project Manager, you must begin by being trustworthy. This means keeping your word, not making promises you can't keep, and informing people right away if something outside of expectations occurs. Trustworthiness is essential in the initial negotiations and contracting for the project, and continues to be central throughout the execution and final delivery of results.

Marcic (1997), like Gibb (1978), asserts that "Trustworthiness becomes the foundation on which all other virtues are based" (48).

She says that without it, without an expectation of truthfulness, all other good behaviors become meaningless.

Judi once worked for a Project Manager on a team that was implementing a major quality and employee involvement program at a Honeywell facility in Arizona. One of the first things he would tell the leaders in the plant was that during the change process, things would get worse before they got better. He said that morale would go down, conflict would increase, and productivity would be negatively affected. He said that he couldn't predict when that would happen, but he could guarantee that it would happen. He told them that we would all do everything we could to mitigate the intensity of the reaction, but that he wasn't going to lie to them and tell them that everything would go smoothly from day one. People knew that he was speaking from experience and that he was telling the truth, and when the expected morale and productivity dip occurred, leaders were able to remain calm, and trusted the team to implement the program professionally.

Becoming more trustworthy requires first becoming more trusting. Gibb (1978) encouraged people to be "as trusting as you can be." This does not mean naively trusting everyone, but it does mean opening yourself up to being more trusting. One of the questions he would encourage clients to consider was, "What would this look like if I (or we) were more trusting?" Secondly, becoming more trustworthy requires competence. It requires attracting the best qualified people to the project team, and investing in whatever skill development they need to do the job well. Marcic writes:

> Let us not forget that the other side of trust is competence. In order for a business to gain trust from customers and suppliers, it must have integrity, as well as be able to perform the job more than adequately. Real trust, then, is integrity times competence. (Marcic 1997: 53)

Albert Schweitzer sums it up beautifully:

Now we must rediscover the fact that we – all together – are human beings, and we must strive to concede to one another what moral capacity we have. Only in this way can we begin to believe that in other peoples as well as ourselves there will arise the need for a new spirit which can be the beginning of a feeling of mutual trustworthiness toward each other. (Schweitzer 1958)

COMMITMENT TO SOMETHING GREATER THAN ONESELF

Daryl Conner is the Chairman of Conner Partners, one of the largest and most successful change management consulting firms in the United States. His organisation received the International Spirit at Work Award in 2007 for their exemplary support for nurturing the human spirit in the workplace. Their consultants are seen by clients as having a great deal of presence, an ineffable sense of being centered and authentic. The organisation consciously hires people who have a commitment to something greater than themselves because they believe that this creates that sense of presence that gives them a competitive edge in the market. Clients want to work with their consultants, even if they can't put words to why they do. The company does not determine what this "something greater than oneself" is. Some might call it God, or Universal Mind, Buddha Nature, Cosmic Consciousness, or some other name, but the key thing is that the person feels a connection to something transcendent that can provide guidance in everyday life and work (Harrington, Conner, and Horney 2000).

In Chapter 1 we talked about the spiritual nature of projects, and the way that project management can provide meaning and purpose to the project team as well as to all the project stakeholders. Anyone who takes on a project large enough to require teamwork is automatically committing to something greater than themselves, even if it is just committing to the team and to a successful conclusion to the project. At the same time, we recognise that self-interest can and does play an important role in project management, and we encourage enlightened self-interest over total selfless service.

However, if you are interested in integrating spirituality into your project management, at the very least, you must have some spiritual relationship to something greater than yourself, whatever you might call that. As Lance Secretan explains, this is the source of "inspired leadership" (Secretan 1999). During the project, you and your team will have many occasions to tap into the Transcendent, if you are open to that source of inspiration and guidance. Out of that connection, you and your team will be able to experience a sense of noble purpose and deep meaning in your work together (Heermann 2004).

PUTTING IT ALL TOGETHER

These six virtues just described are not the only ones that have relevance for project management, but they are a good place to begin. As a Project Manager, you may wish to assess your team on how well these virtues are integrated into your project work. Table 3.2 on the last page of this chapter may be helpful to you. You can use the virtues we have discussed in this chapter, or you can substitute your own. The first step is for you and your team to define what the virtue means to you. Then you can evaluate how well you are living that virtue as a team. Finally, you can identify the virtues that you would like to have more fully integrated in your work and discuss with the team how you can achieve that integration.

SUMMARY

This chapter was designed to provide food for thought about the role of virtues and values in your project management. We reviewed some of the work that authors have done on virtues in the workplace, and pointed out that each author has their own unique list of virtues to offer and each one has different virtues that they think are the core virtues. As you can see, there is no definitive list or model of virtues and it is up to each Project Manager and project team to define for themselves the virtues and values that will guide them in their work together. The next chapter will talk more specifically about the role of spirituality in project management.

Table 3.2   Virtue integration

	We aspire to this virtue. It is not integrated into our work	We live by this virtue most of the time	This virtue is fully integrated into the way our project team operates	Action steps for further virtue integration
Respect for diversity				
Freedom				
Deep listening				
Creativity				
Trustworthiness				
Commitment to something greater than oneself				

CHAPTER 4

THE IMPORTANCE OF SPIRITUALITY IN PROJECT MANAGEMENT

In this chapter we discuss why spirituality is becoming of growing importance in project management. We look at the root causes and how spiritual values and practices are driving changes to the way projects are being established and managed and in particular the role and style of the Project Manager that is increasingly being called for. Spiritual Intelligence (SQ) is a growing requirement particularly on complex mega-projects.

There is a growing use of projects and project management in the world. As more and more people grow out of poverty and rise up the Maslow hierarchy of needs they are reaching the pinnacle of Maslow's pyramid, namely self-actualisation or, as he called it, "spirituality." People want to work on projects that make a difference in the world, and they want work that is meaningful.

So why is Project Management a growing area? Of all the disciplines of management that exist and have been studied, project management is the one that most closely relates to the management of change. As Alvin Toffler observed in his book *Future Shock*, change is accelerating and "change is not merely necessary to life – it is life" (Toffler 1970). He demonstrated this by comparing the many discoveries and inventions, such as the wheel, the Gutenberg press, and computers and the internet, and measuring their existence in human lifetimes. He observed that there was acceleration in terms of human lifetimes of the things that exist and that we use today.

All of us are called to grow and develop to the best of our ability and this includes our body, mind, and spirit. Growth and development require us to take risks and the bigger the risk the more we potentially grow. Projects generally contain a lot of uncertainties at the outset that can be risks both for the project and those engaged in it. Apollo 13 and the Challenger would attest to this. Growth and change are typical of all projects.

There are two types of change in project management: proactive change and reactive change. In proactive change, we are initiating change. Reactive change is where others are launching projects that will have an impact on us and the way in which we work and live, often profoundly so. In fact, much of Toffler's book claimed that there was too much change. He even claimed changes were happening so fast that humankind could not adapt and absorb them. Toffler went on to claim this was devastating for the unprepared, and talked about the stress of people not wanting to fall behind when deciding what to buy or where to go. He observed that technology feeds on knowledge, and knowledge is growing faster than ever. The pace of change is accelerating. New discoveries do not last long; they are disposed of as they are overtaken by new discoveries.

Alan remembers the conception, development, and death of the "Rabbit" phone all in the matter of about five years. When he visited British Telecom's research facility in Martlesham in the late 1980s he was shown a small telephone handset and told we would all soon carry one. Provided we were in range of a Post Office, Railway Station, Bus Station or other civic building we would be able to use the phone which would connect via radio to one of these hubs. We would be able to make a call and the bill would appear on our home phone bill. Sadly, people would be unable to call us back! Judi remembers when her son, who is an early adopter of new technology, carried around a very large and bulky contraption in a large leather case that was the one of the original mobile phones. In a short period of time he traded that in for something much smaller, and then something even smaller.

This idea was overtaken by the rise of the truly mobile phone and later further developments of that technology. When mobile phones were invented, a small by-product was the ability to send text messages. The inventors did not foresee the rise in the use of text. Now the number of text messages exceeds the world population each day. On the internet this year 40 exabytes (40×10^{19}) of unique information will be created, which equals the same amount of unique information created in the last 5,000 years! Toffler saw this pattern emerging in the 1970s and anticipated the shock and stress it would create, especially for the less fortunate being left ever further behind. Some religious folk saw it as a sign of the "end times" but so far they have been proven wrong. The internet now has 2.7 billion searches a month – who answered all these queries before the internet? The book in your hands is one of among 3,000 new books published daily. The manuscript was written on the two authors' laptops and chapters sent back and forth over the internet. This technology is less than 30 years old! Someone has estimated that the sum total of all knowledge is doubling every two years and that soon this will be happening every 72 hours. Will this kind of hyperinflation of knowledge make knowledge valueless as it does money when there is hyperinflation? This huge increase in knowledge is going to have a major impact on education and the way we learn.

Change projects are now initiated in all walks of life including business, government, not-for-profit organisations, education, leisure, and the military. Those that change the way we work or do business can affect us immediately. New products, services, and government projects can change the way we live and may take a little longer before we feel the impact. Projects can be of any size from small to extremely large mega-projects. Their impact on us can also be small or seismic. Perhaps nowhere is more obvious than the use of the internet and e-mail for the search for, and transmission of, information and communications.

Alan's great grandmother, at the age of 17, was put on a sailing ship on the river Clyde and sent to marry his great grandfather in Manila in the Philippines at the end of the nineteenth century. His great grandfather had written home seeking a bride and the negotiations before she was sent would have taken a number of months. The journey itself probably took another three months and we suspect it was at least a year from his decision to find himself a bride to their actual marriage in Manila. She bore him five children. Their great grandson has a Philippine wife. He met his future wife in Hong Kong at the end of the twentieth century when he worked there. They can talk to each other instantaneously by internet or Skype or ordinary landlines, and if they wish to see each other their journey time is a matter of hours and certainly less than a day's travel time in this twenty-first century. All this change in just over a century!

Larger and more complex projects today can be international with project teams drawn from many countries and organisations in order to achieve their objectives. As the complexity grows so does the complexity of the membership of project teams, often formed from disparate groups of people convened for the duration of the project. We see increasing use of virtual teams based miles apart where the members may never be able to meet each other.

One of the most common definitions of spirituality is that which gives meaning and purpose (Mitroff and Denton 1999). Meaning and purpose are becoming an increasingly important part of people's lives as they move up the Maslow hierarchy. Helping project team members to understand the purpose or reason for a project is a major contributor to the effectiveness of the project team. Having a common and understood goal to aim at makes for better projects than those where the goal is unclear which makes it exceptionally hard for the team to form behind. An effective project purpose can do much to inspire the team members. When project team members have a strong sense of meaning and purpose, and a strong alignment around a clear vision, people are able to bring the best of themselves to the project, and even find themselves going beyond what they thought was possible.

A project was started seven years ago in MODEM, a UK charity promoting dialogue between those interested in leadership, organisation, and management, and those interested in theology, spirituality, and ministry. They examined how individuals maintained the energy to undertake tasks and projects that initially they thought very difficult if not impossible. They ran action learning sets and asked the attendees to think of such a project and then talk about how they found the energy to achieve it. The groups were then asked to discuss the examples in their group to see if there was any commonality between them. What they discovered was that the source of this energy was wide and varied but that it usually sat on the spectrum of love at one end and fear at the other. The individuals concerned either seemed to be talking about the leadership and his or her inspirational qualities or similarly the esprit de corps of the team that had formed behind the leader's vision of the project outcome. Sadly, others were driven by fear: fear of failing the leader, the consequences of letting the team down, or being the one to cause the project to fail. There were also people along the spectrum with a variety of other causes from "I heard a voice and knew we would achieve the project," to "suddenly I just knew we would do it!" These are often spirited moments when one feels the presence of a higher power.

We know that the spiritual dimension is growing, and as we observed in Chapter 2, there is now a distinction developing between our spirituality and our faith. For those of a faith it is of course a major influence on the nature of their spirituality and their beliefs and values. However, many younger people who are rather dismissive of faith, not liking the negative things that historically have sprung from religious groups, still believe that they are spiritual and have a growing interest in that aspect of their lives. As Charles Handy described it at an AMBA (Association of MBAs) seminar in London, people need meaning and purpose in their lives and to work in community with others. Projects can provide this in spades. While the old paradigm of work where, as Handy (1994) puts it, people worked for 40 years for one organisation in a number of roles or jobs, nowadays they can have many jobs in life for a variety of employers, undertaking different roles in different organisations. This is never more so than in a project-based career, where people move from project to project and from project team to project team. When people are able to bring the best of themselves to the project this is undoubtedly an inspiring experience and they can find themselves going beyond what they thought possible and achieving something that feels that they are in touch with the transcendent.

We all know or have had the experience of working in a dispirited team, or know others who have, and we know the devastating impact this can have on individual self-esteem and feelings of how we are valued by others. Those of us who have worked in "spirited" teams or organisations know just how uplifting and inspiring that can be too. Georgeanne Lamont studied soul-friendly companies in the UK and found that these organisations consistently had lower absenteeism, less sickness, and lower staff turnover than the national average (Lamont 2002). These kinds of results are also likely for soul-friendly projects.

In dispirited teams the project goals are often unclear or obscure. They may be kept shifting by an uncertain client organisation, or a project sponsor who is unclear what the requirements really are. The "market place" or end users may be repeatedly rapidly changing with new ideas. The rate of change may well then exceed the rate of progress on the project. The project may become endless with no end benefit, no purpose or end in sight. Some team members may leave to find more meaningful projects, and this can have a devastating impact on those left behind. Often this is accentuated because it is the more skilled and resalable members who leave first.

The leadership might change as the original leaders lose the inspiration that they had for the project and/or as they lose the ability to inspire the members of the project team. A Project Manager on a mega-project typically becomes tired or "worn out" in three years and will need replacing in any event. Tremendous planning and sensitivity for the replacement and handover are required if the esprit de corps of the team is to be maintained. If the Project Manager tires and becomes dispirited and moves on, there is further complexity of a handover mid project to a new leader. The uncertainties for the team members become greater as they wonder what the new leader or leadership will be like. The project may well lose momentum and feel like it is going backwards.

Therefore it is exceedingly important to pay attention to the spirit of the team. In a study conducted by Aronson, Shenhar, and Reilly (2010), the authors tested a model of "Project Spirit" to ascertain whether or not higher levels of project spirit are related to project success. Project spirit is defined as the collective attitudes, emotions and norms of behavior that characterise the members of a project team. The model suggests that the Project Manager can undertake activities that build project spirit through instilling a project vision, and through the articulation of values, the creation of social rituals, and the positive use of project team symbols. These "leader instituted spirit building activities" have a positive impact on "spirit expressions" through team members' emotions, attitudes, and behavioral norms, which set the context for performance, leading to project success (Aronson, Shenhar, and Reilly 2010: 3).

Data for the study were collected from 200 core members and Project Managers in 63 projects (Aronson, Shenhar, and Reilly 2010: 5). As hypothesised, the results suggest that leaders building activities affected project members' spirit – defined as "members' emotions, attitudes and norms" (Shenhar, Aronson, and Reilly 2007), which in turn enhanced project outcomes.

> The challenge of achieving exceptional project outcomes appears to relate to the way project leaders integrate the shaping of project spirit as part of their planning activities, with the hard, cold analysis of technology, customers, markets and competitors. (Shenhar et al., 2007)

PERSONALITY TYPOLOGY, TYPES OF INTELLIGENCE, AND PROJECT MANAGEMENT

If a Project Manager is going to be intentional about nurturing the spirit of the project team, it helps if he or she is aware of personality typology and of his or her preferences. We have used the Myers Briggs (MBTI) psychometric model and discovered most Project Managers were ESTJ (Extroverted Sensing Thinking Judging). That is not to say this is the perfect characteristic for team leaders, just an observation of the characteristics that can be helpful in leading project teams. One of Alan's students in the early 1980s did some work using Belbin (2010) and the MBTI models and obtained very high correlations between the results and the performance of the teams. Dr Belbin, when he worked at Henley Management College, arranged the students into teams for a business game. Allegedly he became so good at predicting the results of the business game that they eventually asked him to stop designing the teams.

In the early days of construction projects, teams were often based on the physical prowess of the members and the strongest were often the leaders. We can also see this in early military projects. As the mental work and development of strategy became more important so too the mental aspect of the leadership became more important. IQ became a key trait used to determine who was suitable for higher education. More recently, the work of Goleman (1994) on Emotional Intelligence (EQ) has been seen as a key attribute of good leadership and is a prerequisite for those charged with building effective teams for projects. EQ is the ability to be in touch with our own emotions and to be able to empathise with the feelings of others. This is a key skill for leading and directing teams.

Closely related to Emotional Intelligence is the subject of Spiritual Intelligence (SQ), as first written about by Zohar, a neuro-physicist, and Levin (2001), a journalist and intuitive. Steven Covey observed at a public seminar in London that Spiritual Intelligence is the central and most fundamental of all the intelligences, because it becomes the source of guidance for the others. A number of major companies are using models for developing and measuring Spiritual Intelligence in corporate settings. Companies such as Nokia, Unilever, McKinsey, Shell, Coca-Cola, Hewlett Packard, Merck Pharmaceuticals, Starbucks, and the Co-operative Bank are all quoted in this context.

One such Spiritual Intelligence model has been developed by Cindy Wigglesworth, CEO of Deep Change as mentioned in Chapter 3. She has used her model in a number of organisations in all three sectors

– business, government, and not-for-profit. Spiritual Intelligence is seen as an emergent viable construct within psychology, bolstered particularly by transpersonal psychology, and is receiving considerable scholarship.

Most students of the discipline of project and program[1] management now agree that the key skills for those leading mega-projects are the "softer skills," the interpersonal skills contained within EQ and SQ. Inspirational leadership is a growing requirement for team leaders, both individually and collectively, on major projects and programs (Secretan 2006).

The world is also becoming more conscious of the need for large, highly integrated, and world changing social projects. There is a growing recognition in business of the importance of a social conscience and corporate responsibility. Governments are increasingly recognising their own powerlessness to deal with growing world problems and the need for global business assistance as in many places global business is more powerful and wealthy than the sovereign government. Meanwhile, the human race is facing some very big questions collectively, and at their core are spiritual questions. These questions are of such a scale that they require nations to work together with each other, with business, with not-for-profit organisations and disparate religious organisations.

One way to invite your team to think about the spiritual implications of project management in a generic way is to ask them to discuss the following questions (Table 4.1). This can pave the way for further discussion about specific ways the team might integrate spirituality in their own project.

In order to address these kinds of spiritual questions, leaders will need to develop a greater spiritual intelligence in themselves and in their teams. They will need a global mindset, one that crosses all cultures

---

1   Program management is the management of a collection of projects with similar goals.

Table 4.1   Spiritual questions relevant to Project Management

	Spiritual Question	Our team's thoughts
1.	How do we organise a world where the natural resources are more equitably shared?	
2.	How do we solve the problems with hunger and clean water shortages around the world?	
3.	How do we turn around the problems we face with climate change and global warming?	
4.	How do we respond to natural disasters like tsunamis and earthquakes?	
5.	How do we find and develop technologies to use more sustainable energy sources?	
6.	How do we collectively work to create a sustainable planet?	
7.	Other?	

and understands different cultures and their origins, one that the various faith and spiritual traditions have been teaching for years (Neal 2006). The Judeo-Christian-Islamic tradition teaches us that God is Oneness and we are One with God. Buddhism and Confucianism teach the interconnectedness of all sentient beings. The Baha'i teach that there is one race, the human race. Religious organisations of all the main faiths are also in some cases losing their power and in others growing in power at the more fundamentalist margins. These mega-social projects will need understanding in their leaders and team members to be able to begin to achieve the results the human race so desires.

Spirituality has existed in project management since early historical times and spirituality can be a transformative part of project management if we embrace it more consciously. Human beings are comprised of body, mind, emotion and spirit, and most project management approaches today have focused primarily on the use of the physical (body) and intellectual (mind) aspects of project planning and implementation. More recently, some Project Managers and leaders have seen the value of emotional intelligence, and a few cutting edge leaders are aware of the emerging research and application of spiritual intelligence, particularly for the emerging discipline of managing complex projects (College of Complex Project Managers, and Defence Materiel Organisation 2006).

With a greater understanding of the role of spirituality in project management, program and Project Managers will be able to tap into their team members' passion and purpose, unleash their creativity, and help them solve difficult, seemingly insurmountable problems. They will be able to help their program and project teams develop greater courage to take on problems that seem unsolvable and contribute to projects that truly make a difference in the world.

INTEGRATING SPIRITUALITY AND PROJECT MANAGEMENT

In Part I of this book we provided background information on project management, on spirituality in the workplace and on the virtues and importance of spirituality and project management. In Part II, we provide practical models and tools for integrating spirituality and project management. We start with a focus on the self and spirituality in project management, with the grounding principle that all change must begin with the self. We then move to ways to integrate spirituality and project management first at the team level and then at the organisational level. This book concludes with a discussion of spirituality and project management and the planet, as well as an exploration of the past and future of the field of project management in the context of a spiritual way of looking at things.

CHAPTER 5

SELF AND SPIRITUALITY IN PROJECT MANAGEMENT

In this chapter we consider the self as a spiritual being and examine how this affects the management of projects. We start with the meaning and purpose of life, and the life of self and explore how this affects us as leaders of others. Gibb (1978) coined the term "proximo-distality," which means that change begins with self and expands outward. The Delphi Oracle entrance preached "know thyself." This chapter sets the groundwork for the chapters that follow on spirituality in project teams, spirituality and project management at the organisational level, and spirituality, and project management at the planetary level.

As we said in Chapter 2, "Who am I?" and "Why am I here?" are two of the great questions that most of us have considered at significant turning points in our lives. It is the very answers to these questions that can give us true meaning and purpose for our own lives. They are of course in their essence spiritual questions and many faith groups and religions have spent time and energy exploring them. Fundamentally they are questions about self and spirituality.

They are not easy questions. Psychologists, theologians, and philosophers have pondered these questions for a long time. The importance of nature and nurture in our formation into the persons we become have long been debated as to their relative importance. Was I born like this, or have I developed like this? We now think both contribute to the person we become.

The same longstanding debate applies to leadership qualities and the question, "Are leaders born or made?" Our formation, growth, and development, and the experiences we have during life are all things that shape us into the persons we are. A few years ago, as the Millennium approached, the Cranfield MBA class of 1975 decided to write a book about the members exploring what each one had become and their hopes for the future. Each member was asked to update his CV from the 1975 version, write a paragraph about his family and how they had grown and developed, and a testament to their hopes for the future for themselves, their families, mankind, and the world. The results were fascinating. Most had had interesting careers. Some had risen to great heights and were captains of business, some had become more entrepreneurial and had grown and sold businesses, some becoming wealthy in the process. Most had done reasonably well in material terms and had a high standard of living. The third of the course of 120 members who responded had all had a fascinating quarter century in their work lives, but more interesting was that nearly a third commented that they had engaged in developing their own spirituality. This often expressed itself in their hopes for the future, not just for themselves, but mostly for others – their families and mankind.

Similarly in the 1980s when he taught at Cranfield, Alan was involved in career planning weekends for MBAs and their partners. These followed a pattern of first analysing their pasts, their highs and lows, then their present strengths and weaknesses, their opportunities and their threats, their values and their relative importance. Then they would look to the future – their hopes and aspirations and desired achievements in the next five years, ten years and a normal lifetime. Finally they were asked to consider the future and what it would look like if they only had a year to live. The most interesting thing was how often these stereotyped high flyers with personal aspirations for money and wealth would reveal in this final futuristic exercise their deep felt desires to be philanthropic, to help others and to achieve things of little or no benefit to themselves. It was a truly uplifting experience to hear them express such desires with such passion and feeling. These were projects that gave them meaning and purpose in their lives. Likewise we have seen many Project Managers stepping forward to work on pro bono projects for charities at home and abroad. This seems to bring a real sense of fulfilment to the Project Managers doing this vital work. As Jesus would say, "What you do unto the least of these, you do for me."

Almost all leadership writers and theorists agree that great leaders first and foremost know themselves. Spiritual leaders make the same comment about studying spirituality. Jesus in his summary of the commandments calls us first to love God and secondly to love our neighbour as our self. This is of course not unique to Christianity as most of the great faiths or religious traditions echo this second commandment. The importance here is that to love others we have to first love our self and this requires us to know our self.

As Howard and Welbourn state:

> [S]pirituality helps us in our struggle to determine who we are (our being) and how to live our lives in this world (our doing). We call ourselves human beings but more often than not when asked about ourselves we talk about our doings – a paradox ... It combines our basic philosophy towards life, our vision and our values, with our conduct and practice. Spirituality encompasses our ability to tap into our deepest resources, that part of ourselves which is unseen and mysterious, to develop our fullest potential. It also sets alive our web of relationships as we look outward in order to make meaningful connections and help others achieve their fullest potential. Both this inward and outward journey gives us the opportunity to discover and articulate our personal meaning and purpose in life. On the way we are able to learn about love, joy, peace, creative fulfilment and how to live expectantly with a sense of vitality and abundance. But we also encounter suffering, moral ambiguity, and personal fear. It is our spirituality, providing as it does a deeper identity, which guides us as we chart our way through life's paradoxes. (Howard and Welbourn 2004: 35)

But as we have seen in previous chapters spirituality is hard to define in absolute terms – it is in part a mystery. According to Howard and Welbourn (2004) definitions center around three areas:

- the basic feeling about being connected with one's complete self (body, mind, emotion and spirit), others and the entire universe;

- underlying principles, e.g. virtues, ethics, values, emotions, wisdom and intuition;

- the relationship between a personal inner experience and its positive manifestations in outer behaviors, principles and practices.

As Matthew Fox, a famous US Episcopalian priest, says:

> *Spirituality is a life filled path, a spirit way of living ... A path is the way itself and every moment on it is a holy moment; a sacred seeing goes on there. (Fox 1994)*

In MODEM's research they discovered that people seem to fall loosely into two groups. They all distinguish between spirit with a little "s," the spirit in each one of us (as in we are made up of body, mind, and spirit) and the Spirit with capital "S," meaning that Spirit from a higher power, the Spirit of God to some of us. All who took part in the research agreed on little "s." Big "S" was more divisive, splitting groups in two, those who had an experience of the transcendent and those who did not know what the other group were talking about! (Pettifer 2002). The factors that support the increase of spiritual energy in the workplace were:

1. *An inspiring purpose – something achievable and worthwhile and which the participants found to be stretching and requiring special effort.*
2. *A liberating and empowering context – one in which the participants were free to take decisions, to develop their potential and to work creatively with others.*
3. *An attitude of hope, confidence and commitment – readiness to seize opportunities. (Pettifer 2002: 3)*

Dermot Tredget, a monk and priest at Douai Abbey, a Benedictine monastery in England, who runs courses on spirituality in the workplace and founded a meeting group of the same name there with David Welbourn (now numbering more than 80 members), said at one of the meetings that Spirituality involves:

- growth;

- becoming a person in the fullest sense;

- conversion and *metanoia* (a fundamental shift in mind in which individuals come to see themselves as capable of creating the world they truly want, rather than reacting to circumstances beyond their control);

- relationships (vertical and horizontal);

- attitudes, beliefs and practices;

- the intellect, emotions and the soul.

What seems to be becoming clearer is that if we wish to be better than average project leaders we first need to know our selves, our whole selves – body, mind, emotion, and spirit.

We can find out more about our *body* by testing it in the gym or some other sporting activity. This can be done solo or in a team game. There is an increasing interest in living healthier lives, particularly as work becomes a more sedentary activity and as we learn much more about our bodies than we once knew. We need to feed properly, eating and drinking things that are good for us and limiting the quantities of the things we now know are less good for us. We need to tune our bodies so they are at their best, and we can do this through exercise and training. We know we should do exercise regularly and for a minimum of 30 minutes at least four times a week. From a spiritual perspective, our bodies are the divine temples of our soul and need to be cared for.

We can exercise our *minds*, and many of us do so through work and play. We use our brains to create new ideas and projects and to plan them before doing them. We acquire knowledge and put it into use to understand it and with experience and reflection we may convert it into wisdom that we can use again. Reading books and searching the internet can help us in this endeavor. Formal studies and accreditations can help us test our knowledge, understanding, and experience. Alan chairs a company that is exclusively focused on developing qualifications and accrediting people in Project Management capabilities. This currently seems to be a real growth industry as many more of us progress from project to project and from employer to employer and need certifications as one way of demonstrating our suitability for undertaking the next task or role.

We know more about our *emotions* through the work of Goleman (1994) and others. We can increase our understanding by knowing our own feelings and gauging the feelings of others. As we collectively increase our abilities to express our feelings, to explore them, and to share them, so we are in a better position to understand and support each other when individuals go through difficult times emotionally. We all know it is harder to focus on our work when we are emotionally disturbed. We need balanced emotions at home, work and play to fully contribute to teamwork on projects. When we are distracted by our emotions in other areas we need the support of our team members to help us through the difficult times. Of course the knowing self is better able to accept the support of others in difficult times and not see it as a personal weakness.

There are many practices that we can adopt from the worlds of Psychology and Organisational Behavior to learn more about ourselves and others and group behavior.

We need to know more about our *spirit* and to know ourselves spiritually if we are to be complete and to play a full part in the teams we work with. We can do this by learning to use various spiritual tools and practices such as reflection, silence, prayer, and meditation. These help us to carry issues into our deeper self and to reflect on them in order to discern the best solution. These practices also develop our self-awareness, which can help us to be more aware of others. This can help us when we work with others to show true understanding and offer support in their development and growth.

As mentioned earlier, a survey by the Chartered Management Institute in the UK discovered that what most of us want from our immediate boss is authenticity. We want to work for someone who is consistent and can be known since they are genuine and prepared to share of themselves. Our ego is an important part of the self. In childhood as we develop and grow we build up our ego. We protect our egos in order to build ourselves up. However, as we grow in spirit, and as spiritual teachers demonstrate, we should learn to diminish our ego. This will enable us to dominate less, to put ourselves at the service of others, and to truly practice servant leadership. This will help us to learn to build up others and to support them rather than ourselves, in practice to become truly authentic servant leaders (Greenleaf 1977). We learn to distinguish between the narrow ego self and the greater Self that we have it within us to become. Some describe the process of meditation as an emptying of self (ego) to discover the real me within. Gandhi is reported to have said that when he had a small issue or problem he meditated for an hour or two, and when he had a major problem he could spend all day meditating on it. He called us all to be the change we want to see in the world. It is easier to change yourself than the other person! And yet so often we find ourselves wanting to change other people.

You may wish to do a personal assessment with how satisfied you are with your development in these four human domains. You can use the form in Table 5.1 on the following page to ask yourself how satisfied you are with your development in these areas and what, if anything, you might want to do to improve your personal and professional growth in this area.

You may also wish to do this kind of assessment with your entire project team, with the question in mind about the ways in which the project helps or hinders your collective development in each of the four domains (see Table 5.2).

Table 5.1 Personal grid for four domains

	Dissatisfied: I need a lot of development in this area	Moderately Satisfied: I need some work in this area	Very Satisfied: I can help others develop in this area	Actions I could take to develop this domain more fully
Physical				
Mind				
Emotional				
Spiritual				

Table 5.2 Team grid for four domains

	This project could have a negative impact on the development of this domain for team members	This project could have a neutral impact on the development of this domain	This project could have a positive impact on the development of this domain for team members	Actions our team could take to develop this domain more fully
Physical				
Mind				
Emotional				
Spiritual				

After the journey to discover self, the "who am I?" question, another key question is "why am I here?" or "what is my purpose?," "what should I be doing?" For many this leads us to the world of work, or as Fox (1994) put it, to our "sacred work." What is work for? It is our endeavor to participate in creation with our God or Higher Power. We live in a wonderful world created out of nothing. This world we live in sustains us and we need to sustain it.

Work, as anyone who has ever been made redundant knows, provides dignity and an income. Alan was once working on a North Sea oil rig yard in the North East of England in Hartlepool. The yard built three deep sea oil production platforms in what was once Europe's largest dry dock in the 1970s when the rest of the UK was on a three-day week. These were floated out into the North Sea to become production platforms for North Sea oil. Laing Offshore, the main contractor building the platforms, employed more than 5,000 people directly and probably the same again as sub-contractors or local suppliers to build each platform. Those 10,000 people then indirectly provided more local employment for the goods and services that they purchased with their wages. It was a major part of the local economy. When the third and final platform was floated out all these people were made redundant. While there was a good terminal bonus paid at the end as redundancy, it did not go far, as the other major industries in the North East closed down. The shipyards were now a shadow of their former selves, the coal pits were shut, the ICI Chemical Works were doing much less than they once did, and more recently the Corus Steel Plant on Teeside shut down its furnaces for the last time and paid off its skilled workforce. All this had a devastating impact on the local area. Many men who were used to jobs in heavy industry are now unemployed, and their self-esteem has fallen to a very low ebb. It is quite clear that work is important for all of us and our well-being.

Projects in all sectors provide much needed work for people. Some project team members will have to retrain to develop new skills to match the needs of the newer industries, but that is much better than the alternative of unemployment and hopelessness. In some places we now have more than one generation that have never had work.

Projects can undoubtedly supply sacred work. All projects invariably involve people, usually lots of them. Each person who is going to work on a project has to be briefed about their particular work package that goes to make up the whole. As Wilber (2001) says, we break things down from the whole into the constituent parts to more easily understand the part we have to play, but as he reminds us we need to remember the whole and what he calls holons. People who work on small parts of projects need to be informed about the overall purpose of the project and where their part fits into the whole.

A NASA scientist whose job was to work on the tiles used to protect the Shuttle on its re-entry to the earth found it hard to realise the purpose that the tile played in enabling the Shuttle, or "truck" as it was nicknamed, in carrying the materials into space to build a space station. Further flights could be launched from the space station to reach into outer space – a far greater goal and so much easier to feel good about. We now understand the importance of the tile after some were dislodged during takeoff of the Challenger craft, leading to the destruction of the shuttle during its re-entry and the death of the astronauts.

We use many project management processes in managing projects. Typical processes include:

- define the project;

- determine the business case (why we are doing it);

- define the scope (what we are doing);

- determine the plan (how we are going to do it);

- the work breakdown structure (or product breakdown in PRINCE2®);

- define all the elements (work packages) that make up the whole project scope;

- the cost estimate for each work package and the total project estimate;

- the time schedule for each work package;

- the network showing the logical order for undertaking each project activity and work package;

- the critical path and hence the overall timescale for the project;

- the iterative process to match the business case and the plan.

All too often the process becomes an end in itself rather than a tool to help the overall project. The project management process should be a means to an end and not an end in itself. Indeed the project itself is a means to an end and not an end in itself. It is not until we put the outputs of the project to use that the benefits used to justify the investment in the project begin to flow and pay back that investment. In point of fact the importance of many of these processes is the team involved working through the process rather than the output it produces. All too often we forget this and focus on ticking off the outputs of the various processes, rather than looking at how well the process has been done; whether those who are going to do the work were involved; how committed they are to the plan (do they believe it or not?); and whether they will work hard to achieve it.

PEOPLE ISSUES

If the people involved are to understand the overall purpose they need it explained, however small their part. It is this purpose that can give the individual that meaning and purpose in life that feeds their spirituality; the making sense of life, work, and why we are here. The same is true for each of their colleagues on the project; when each and every individual has their own sense of the meaning and purpose of the project they will be able to develop a meaning and purpose for the whole team. Jaworski (1997) uses the "wilderness experience" to help potential leaders to discover themselves and meditate on project work. The wilderness experience is leaving people, on their own, in the wilderness for a minimum of 24 hours. There are of course other ways to develop our individual spirituality. This may be through reading books such as this one, or ones on the subject of meditation and contemplation; practising a form of meditation on a regular basis and expanding this when dealing with problems; or learning to apply deep listening to other individuals. We may want to tap our other attributes for feelings and spirituality through listening to our intuition. We may learn how to be better in touch with our intuition. Richard Olivier, son of Sir Laurence, uses drama exercises to help people develop their intuition, such as:

- the group walking randomly in a room and learning to stop and start simultaneously with no signal, purely learning to sense when they are all going to stop, or move again;

- the group forming a triangular phalanx with the person in the front setting the direction and movement forwards until he turns through 60 degrees and a new person is at the front and leads the group – again with no sound or visible warning of the change in direction and leadership;

- the group standing in a circle and counting from the number one to the number of the group total, say 20. They are to count randomly, without duplication or repetition, up to 20. At the outset it seems impossible and then eventually the group achieves it with a great sense of elation.

Discussion afterwards about how it was achieved will lead the group to understand the power of individual intuition. Through awareness of others, developed in silence, we can pick up their vibrations and learn even more about them.

We have used the outdoors with its real dramas and situations to help people on their voyage of self-discovery, often through feedback from the other individuals in group exercises requiring trust, support and discovering the diversity of talents in the group.

Eventually things develop into patterns rather than one-time random events, and the patterning helps participants to add a new set of skills to their decision making, and to become more attuned to other individuals. When all our senses are working and tuned in to the group we realise we are as one; we have come together.

COMPETENCIES

As project management has developed as a management science, one key area that has developed is the delineation of competencies. In the early days, the first competencies to be recognised were the technical project management skills – a good understanding of the overall process and the individual processes and procedures that led there. These became known by their professional membership bodies as the Body of Knowledge (BoK). The Project Management Institute (PMI), originally formed in the US but now operating worldwide with Chapters in most countries, has always been recognised as a process based BoK. In the UK, the BoK of the Association for Project Management is also a set of process-oriented topics. Interestingly, the International Project Management Association's lead document is the International Competence Baseline (ICB). Most of these BoKs and the ICB are beginning to add further areas and competencies such as: interpersonal skills (sometimes referred to as soft skills), skills related to the particular sector or project environment (what Belbin (2010) would call the "Specialist" role), team building and leadership skills, and perhaps most important of all, the ability to integrate these into the whole.

The good Project Manager or leader needs a number of these attributes to increase the likelihood of a successful project. The harder thing is finding them all in one person – tenacity, drive, foresight, planning, team building, motivation, persuasion, excellent interpersonal skills with strong belief in the project vision. These soft skills are even more important in program managers and senior management and directors.

Successful leaders are the ones who get things done – who achieve. There are endless books on leadership and leadership styles and many disagree about the right attributes of successful leaders – one theorist even claimed that the best leaders all had wide-set eyes! (Kippenberger 2002). Most of this search for common attributes of great leaders has now been dismissed as untrue. However, there is some agreement that leaders take us through change to their (and our) shared vision for the future; while managers manage the status quo (Harpham and Kippenberger 2006).

Nonetheless it is almost impossible for the BoKs or ICB to identify every single competence that every project or program manager would need for every conceivable program or project. Dombkins (2007) discusses the competences of program and Project Managers for complex mega-projects. Many of the competences he points at would fall under the EQ category. Many of the competences that Dombkins identifies as being necessary for Projam Managers (projam is his invented word for complex program and Project Managers) are also recognisable as SQ skills or Spiritual Intelligence skills. These include creativity, innovative thinking, inspiring others, reflectiveness, servant leadership, and many others (Zohar and Marshall 2000).

Also essential are the relationships with the sponsors or clients who are generally paying for the project and carrying the vision. The good Project Manager needs to understand the vision and be able to empathise with the sponsors, help them make timely decisions, and suggest options and ways around road blocks on the project path (Conner 1993).

ORGANISING

Before organising the project team, the effective Project Manager first will want to get him or herself properly organised. Generally this begins by making sure that they know "why" the project is being done – this should help them understand or develop the vision for the project. The Project Manager can use this to inspire him or herself to deliver the outcome seen in the vision. Project Managers need also to ask the sponsor for the business case for the project used to justify the organisation's investment in it. The PM then needs to agree with the sponsor the "what" of the project. The scope of what is to be included and excluded. The final step is for the PM to develop the "how," how much and when – the plan for the execution of the project. This is often done initially by the PM and sponsor using the project team. This will therefore be covered in more depth in Chapter 6.

STAKEHOLDERS

Finally, relationships must be built with all the stakeholders. A stakeholder is anyone with a vested interest in the outcome of the project. Some will be powerful and influential, some weak with little influence. Some will support the project and its intended outcome, others may be strongly opposed to it and its likely outcomes. The more the project sits in the public domain or is politically inspired the more likelihood of involved stakeholders. While the Project Manager has processes to identify stakeholders and where they stand, he or she must determine the best way to inform and influence them, and to form authentic, trusting relationships that say we can work together even when we do not agree.

Many of these relationships will be initiated and maintained by the PM. For example, the sponsor relationship as well as some other key stakeholders, particularly the more individualistic ones. Others will be maintained more corporately and these will be covered in Chapter 6.

People respect the authentic project leader who tells it as it is. The best project leaders first know themselves and have a good understanding of all their stakeholders.

SUMMARY

In order to integrate spirituality and project management, the central focus needs to be on the self, and on the spiritual development or formation of the individual. The self is the initial building block. This chapter extends from earlier chapters the discussion of the importance of meaning and purpose in project management as it relates to individuals, and offers a connection with Emotional Intelligence (EQ) and Spiritual Intelligence (SQ). Many of the competences of project management benefit from the development of EQ and SQ. If individuals are the basic building block of spirituality and project management, then teams are the next building block. The next chapter looks at the ways in which teams might integrate a more spiritual approach to working together on projects.

CHAPTER 6

TEAMS AND SPIRITUALITY IN PROJECT MANAGEMENT

All human beings are spiritual beings. As we described in Chapter 5, it is important as a Project Manager to know one's self, one's whole self – body, mind, emotion, and spirit. In this chapter we explore the ways in which spirituality is experienced at the team level in project teams. If each individual is a spiritual being, then there is the potential for collective spiritual energy when people come together. And it is just as important for a project team to know itself – to have self-awareness about the body, mind, emotion, and spirit of the team as a whole. There are many books about team building that focus on developing relationships and team skills, but they tend to ignore the spiritual dimension of teams. Katzenback and Smith (2003), for instance, describe High Performance Teams as having the following key characteristics: complementary skills, mutual accountability, common approach, and shared goals. These are all necessary but not sufficient characteristics of spirit in project teams. High Performance Teams are teams that develop a deep personal commitment among the members of the team for one another's personal growth and wellbeing while rising to concrete and measurable challenges. In this chapter we go one step further to describe teams where the Project Manager and team members are committed to one another's spiritual growth and to making a positive difference in the world.

Jesus said, "Where two or three are gathered in my name, there I am" (Matthew 18:20). Hindus gather together in Satsang, or spiritual community, as an important part of evolving in their consciousness. Native Americans gather in Wisdom Councils for spiritual guidance about major decisions that affect the tribe and future generations. All of the wisdom traditions have spiritual practices that incorporate a group of people coming together for some higher purpose. Each of these traditions has something to offer to project teams that truly want to tap into the deeper dimensions of meaning, purpose, and commitment to the project.

Project management provides an individual the opportunity to find greater spirituality in his or her life through being involved in something that brings greater meaning and purpose, and through the challenges and opportunities for personal growth that are provided by relationships. The most effective project management teams are the ones that understand the balance between the discipline of process on the one hand and the valuing of relationships and spiritual connection on the other.

By taking a spiritual approach to project team development and leadership, individual team members benefit in their own spiritual development, and the project stakeholders benefit because team members are more committed, inspired, and effective in implementing the processes needed for a successful project completion.

There are five approaches that a PM might consider when leading project management teams in a spiritual way:

1. Alignment: Aligning vision, meaning, and purpose at the team level.
2. Spiritual leadership: Seeing oneself as a Servant Leader to the team and being committed to helping each team member be a Servant Leader to others.
3. Esprit de corps: Understanding and honouring the collective spirit of the team.
4. Communication: Using non-traditional communication methods as a way of building trust and openness.
5. Creativity: Recognising that inspiration comes from Spirit, and utilising group spiritual practices from the wisdom traditions to support inspired problem solving.

Each of these approaches will be described briefly, and examples of activities and processes you might use in your project team will be offered.

ALIGNMENT
Aligning vision, meaning, and purpose at the team level

In order to align vision, meaning, and purpose within your project management team, you, as PM, must first be clear about your own vision for the project, and what its meaning and purpose is for you in your own life and work. It is important to communicate your vision and to be willing to share on a personal level how this project provides meaning and purpose to you. You also need to communicate what the meaning and purpose of the project is to the stakeholders. The more you can state this in terms of virtues and values (see Chapter 3), the better.

The next step is to create alignment within the team, and in order to do this, you must be open to having your vision and meaning and purpose enhanced by what others in the team have to say. One process for creating alignment is to bring people together for an Alignment Session and to ask them to each write a brief story about a project they worked on in the past that provided them a strong sense of meaning and purpose. Stories are a time-honored tradition for evoking spiritual wisdom. Next, put them in small groups of three to five people to share their stories, and ask people to listen for the themes and similarities. Have people collect these themes on flip charts or through decision software. Once each group has completed their list of themes regarding meaning and purpose, ask for two or three volunteers to tell the entire group a little bit about their story of a project where they felt a strong sense of meaning and purpose. Then list all the themes on a white board or other data collection method that is visible to the entire group. Finally, lead a discussion with full participation, to discuss what each person's vision is for the project and how this project can create a collective experience of meaning and purpose for the team. The following chart (Table 6.1) might be useful in documenting the stories and the themes.

Table 6.1   Creating alignment around meaning and purpose

Team Member	Story of project with meaning and purpose	Themes from the story	How this project can create meaning and purpose
A			
B			
C			
D			
E			

A very different kind of alignment process you could use is based on the Native American process of vision questing (Neal 2006). When you are kicking your project off in a project management planning retreat, select a retreat location where team members have access to nature, whether that be gardens, a forest, or seashore. After sharing your personal vision, meaning and purpose, as described above, invite team members to spend time in nature, reflecting on their personal vision, meaning, and purpose for the project. At a minimum, you should schedule at least one hour for them to be in nature, and one hour for processing their experience.

In your instructions for their vision quest, ask them to look to nature for symbols and messages. Remind them that in all wisdom traditions, spiritual leaders from time immemorial have gone into nature for guidance from God. A vision quest is the process of seeking a vision and asking for guidance from the spiritual world about the purpose and meaning of what you are about to undertake. It helps if each person brings a journal, and you can suggest that if they receive a message from nature, they can bring back a symbol of that message.

When people return, assemble them in a circle for a wisdom council meeting. Each person shares something about their experience and the message they brought back, knowing that the message is not just for them, but for the community that is the project team.

The former CEO of Rockport Shoes, Angel Martinez, is a very spiritual man and took a spiritual approach to the way he ran the business. As a result of his inspired leadership, the company did a major turnaround from losing a lot of money to becoming one of the most profitable businesses in the shoe industry. The company was growing and needed a new corporate headquarters. Mr Martinez shared his vision of the company culture as being one that nurtured the artist within. At a project planning retreat for the design of the new headquarters, each of the top managers of the organisation was asked to take a camera and to go into nature for one hour to look for a symbol or message of what the new corporate headquarters should be like. When the managers returned, they loaded their photos onto a computer and each person showed one or two photos and talked about their photo of a rock, leaf, bird or stone, provided a vision for what they would like to see in the corporate headquarters and how they would like the new design to support the organisational culture. The Vice-President of Human Resources pulled all their ideas together and that collective vision created the basis for the architectural plans of the new building. Thomas Merton, the famous Trappist contemplative monk of the Abbey of Gethsemane, also used photographs to capture images of the God within (De Waal 1992).

SPIRITUAL LEADERSHIP

Seeing oneself as a Servant Leader to the team, and being committed to helping each team member be a Servant Leader to others

There are many different models of spiritual leadership, and one of the most popular of these is Servant Leadership based on a framework developed by Robert Greenleaf (1977), who was a retired executive from AT&T. He developed this model after reading Hermann Hesse's spiritual tale, titled *The Journey to the East* (1932). He offers this test of whether or not someone is a servant leader:

> *Do those served grow as persons; do they while being served become healthier, wiser, freer, more autonomous, more likely themselves to become servants? (Greenleaf 1977)*

Larry Spears, the former Director of the Greenleaf Center for Servant Leadership, identified 10 characteristics of a servant leader. Several of these characteristics are quite spiritual in nature. For example, one characteristic is awareness, especially self-awareness, which is central to all the major religious traditions (Spears 1998). Contemplative practices such as prayer, meditation, and journaling are powerful tools for self-awareness.

Another characteristic is commitment to the growth of people, with a belief that people have an intrinsic value beyond their tangible contribution as workers. This is also one of the key characteristics of an effective PM. Leaders who exhibit this characteristic are high in spiritual intelligence (Wigglesworth 2010).

When teams climb major mountains like Everest, only a few members of the overall team reach the top, but it is the whole team who feel the sense of accomplishment. Likewise, when a racing driver wins in Formula One, it is the whole team who share in that sense of being first or winning. Alan's son, Richard, had the privilege of managing the Ghanaian Ski Team in the 2010 Winter Olympics in Whistler. The team comprised one skier, Kwame, the snow leopard, who participated in the slalom. He came 47th out of 104 entrants and achieved more than he had hoped for. His team of four – the manager, the ski coach, the fitness coach, and the internet expert – all shared in his sense of a personal victory. We were pleased that they each received a medal for their participation in helping Kwame to be there and to do as well as he did. All of the backup teams at the Olympics share this real sense of lasting recognition for their achievement.

One of the key skills for any project leader is the ability to build relationships that work and enable alliances for the benefit of the project. The relationships with the key project team members are essential for building and maintaining a trusting, compact team who work well together, support each other, go the extra mile for each other and can deliver even when the going gets tough. The PM needs to be able to inspire them to even greater levels of performance.

Fry (2003, 2005) has done extensive research on spiritual leadership and has developed a causal model demonstrating the relationship between:

1. spiritual leadership values, attitudes and behaviors;
2. follower needs for spiritual survival; and
3. organisational outcomes.

His research shows that vision, hope/faith, and altruistic love lead to organisational commitment, productivity, ethical and spiritual wellbeing, and corporate social responsibility. For team leaders who wonder if there is a business case for spiritual leadership, it is well worth it to read Fry's work. It will inspire you to be the kind of spiritual leader your heart may be calling you to be.

One of the best ways to develop your spiritual leadership strength is to work with a spiritual business coach or a spiritual director. Many workplace chaplains have the skills to be a spiritual business coach, or you may want to contact the Tyson Center for Faith and Spirituality in the Workplace to use one of their coaches. The coach may have you take a self-assessment instrument such as the Spiritual Intelligence Questionnaire (Wigglesworth 2010), the Spiritual Leadership Survey (Fry 2005), or the Edgewalker Assessment (Neal and Hoopes 2011). The coach will work with you to define your vision of what spiritual leadership looks like for you and will guide you on developing your capabilities. There are also many courses and workshops on spiritual leadership development that can be helpful.

ESPRIT DE CORPS
Understanding and honouring the collective spirit of the team

Each of us has at one time or another been on a project team where there was an incredible sense of esprit de corps. Those experiences are quite memorable and are probably one of the major reasons people are interested in joining project teams. Esprit de corps is defined as "the common spirit existing in the members of a group and inspiring enthusiasm, devotion, and strong regard for the honor of the group" (Merriam-Webster). Literally it means "spirit of the group."

A team is a living system, and each living system has its own spirit. Just as we each have our own spirit and must consciously do things to nourish that spirit, a team must consciously do things to nourish the spirit of the team. Barry Heermann developed a program called Team Spirit (1997) that incorporates organisational development practices, group dynamics processes, and knowledge from the wisdom traditions of the world. Team Spirit has a six phase Team Spirit Spiral with activities at every stage, all of which center around service. Heermann and his colleagues have learned over time that the thing that distinguishes teams with esprit de corps and high performance from average or low performing teams is the focus on service to each other and to the customer or stakeholder.

You might consider conducting a "Customer Service Analysis" with your team. This approach begins with identifying your internal and external customers. Your internal customers are your fellow members on the project team. Your external customers are those who are paying for the project, your vendors, and other external stakeholders. For each customer, you define what "service" means to them. In your definition, include their expectations of the project team, and also include what gives them meaning and purpose. You can adapt this grid (Table 6.2) for your particular project.

From this analysis, you can begin to see a pattern of expectations and of what provides a sense of meaning and purpose to both the internal and external customers. The team can then discuss what it means to be of service in this project. They may decide to find a way to measure customer satisfaction with their service, which can be very helpful and could be a key KPI (key performance indicator) for the project.

One of the phases of the Team Spirit Spiral is "celebration." This is an important focus that is often not considered by many PMs. A unique example of celebration occurs in Pfizer's drug development project teams. Like other teams, they celebrate their successes on a regular

Table 6.2   Customer service analysis grid

Internal Customers	Expectations of Project	Meaning and Purpose of this Project
Team Leader		
Team Member A		
Team Member B		
Team Member C		
Admin Assistant		
Other		

External Customers	Expectations of Project	Meaning and Purpose of this Project
Client		
Vendor A		
Vendor B		
Government Inspector		
Site Manager		
Other		

Table 6.3   Team role analysis

Team Role	Definition	This role is not natural to me	Play this role sometimes	This role comes naturally and easily
Plant	Are needed to be highly creative and good at solving problems in unconventional ways. The role was so-called because one such individual was "planted" in each team			
Monitor Evaluator	Are needed to provide a logical eye, make impartial judgments where required and to assess the team's options in a dispassionate way.			
Coordinators	Are needed to focus on the team's objectives, draw out team members and delegate work appropriately.			
Shaper	Are needed to vigorously, and even aggressively, pursue objectives, 'shaping' and challenging others.			

Table 6.3   Continued

Team Role	Definition	This role is not natural to me	Play this role sometimes	This role comes naturally and easily
Resource Investigators	Provide inside knowledge on the opposition and made sure that the team's idea would carry to the world outside the team.			
Implementers	Are needed to plan a practical, workable strategy and carry it out as efficiently as possible.			
Completer Finishers	Are most effectively used at the end of a task, to "polish" and scrutinise the work for errors, subjecting it to the highest standards of quality control.			
Teamworkers	Help the team to gel, using their versatility to identify the work required to complete it on behalf of the team.			
Specialist	Have in-depth knowledge of a key area.			

basis. But they also celebrate their failures, when their research shows that a drug line they were working on does not have any potential to improve medical conditions. They celebrate the closing down of that line of research because they learned important things from their experiments and because resources are now freed up to follow more promising drug compounds. As you can imagine, there is a very high sense of esprit de corps in these teams. Lamont (2002) describes a similar form of celebration of failure at Happy Computers, where the CEO shows up with a bottle of champagne when someone discovers something that could fail and it has.

As the project team develops milestones in their project planning, we encourage you to incorporate milestone celebrations. These need not be expensive and time-consuming events, and are often most meaningful when they are designed by the project team members themselves.

Another approach to developing esprit de corps is to understand the different roles each project team needs in order to be effective and then to learn about the team member's natural gifts in these areas so that all the roles are fulfilled. Theories abound about team building and acceleration of the process of team members' getting to know each other and their individual strengths and weaknesses. Belbin (2010) has done much on the roles team members play and how each individual has an affinity to a particular role. Most Project Managers are what Belbin calls *shapers* with the drive and energy to keep the team moving forwards without losing focus or momentum. Belbin highlighted the need for the team to have a cross section of other abilities. Your team may wish to evaluate itself on these different roles. Each person can use the form in Table 6.3 to rate themselves on the roles they play in the team, and then the information can be combined to evaluate whether or not any roles are missing or are overrepresented.

It was only after the initial research had been completed that the ninth Team Role, *Specialist* emerged. The simulated management exercises in Belbin's research had been deliberately set up to require no previous knowledge. In the real world, however, the value of an individual with in-depth knowledge of a key area came to be recognised as yet another essential team contribution or Team Role. Like the other Team Roles, Specialists also have a weakness: a tendency to focus narrowly on their own subject of choice, and to prioritise this over the team's progress.

One role Belbin did not identify is that of the "Prima Donna," a role that plays havoc with the team dynamics, as indeed can some "specialists." The trick is to try to not make them team members but to keep them outside the team as an adviser or consultant to the team.

The purpose of psychological models such as Belbin's is not to think that you can build the perfect team, but rather that you need to seek a balanced team with each of these properties or characteristics being undertaken by a member of the team and not putting too many people in the team with the same characteristics leading to dispiriting competition over leadership.

COMMUNICATION
Using non-traditional communication methods as a way of building trust and openness

All good PMs are very clear about traditional methods of communicating the goals of a project, the deliverables, and the expectations about deadlines and costs. This is necessary but not sufficient for leading project management teams from a more profound spiritual place. If you really want to tap into the spiritual energy and wisdom of a team, you will need to add some non-traditional communication methods to your skill set.

One of these communication methods is Bohmian Dialogue (Bohm, Nichol, and Senge 2004). This is a method of developing deeper self-awareness and team consciousness in a group of people, and does not have a specific agenda or task outcome. The purpose is to develop a deeper level of listening to the group's collective wisdom. David Bohm was a quantum physicist who became interested in philosophy, thought as a system, and the need for a shift in consciousness to help solve the fragmentation experienced by most people.

There are four principles of Bohmian Dialogue:

1. **The group agrees that no group-level decisions will be made in the conversation.**
   In the dialogue group we are not going to decide what to do about anything. This is crucial. Otherwise we are not free. We must have an empty space where we are not obliged to anything, nor to come to any conclusions, nor to say anything or not say anything. It's open and free. It's an empty space.

2. **Each individual agrees to suspend judgment in the conversation.**
   (Specifically, if the individual hears an idea he doesn't like, he does not attack that idea.) People in any group will bring to it assumptions, and as the group continues meeting, those assumptions will come up. What is called for is to suspend those assumptions, so that you neither carry them out nor suppress them. You don't believe them, nor do you disbelieve them; you don't judge them as good or bad.

3. **As these individuals "suspend judgment" they also simultaneously are as honest and transparent as possible.**
   Specifically, if the individual has a "good idea" that he might otherwise hold back from the group because it is too controversial, he will share that idea in this conversation.

4. **Individuals in the conversation try to build on other individuals' ideas in the conversation.**
   The group often comes up with ideas that are far beyond what any of the individuals thought possible before the conversation began) (Bohm, Nichol, and Senge 2004: 18–22)

Bohmian Dialogue is used when logic and analysis have run up against their limitations and a project management team needs to create something it does not know how to do. This is a form of conversation that is meant to be generative rather than problem solving. The Project Manager can instruct team members to use open-ended questions as much as possible, such as "Tell me more about that," or "What is it about this situation that touches you," or "What are you sensing, even if you have no evidence?"

Judi participated in a Bohmian dialogue session that was used for new product development in a small business. The facilitator directed the group to listen to the soul of the group rather than to speak for oneself. More importantly, the group was advised to listen deeply and with full focus on the speaker without trying to think about what you were going to say in response. This type of listening, and letting go of ego, allows for inspiration to arise, and the group ended up coalescing with great excitement and energy around a new product that none of them had expected to create.

Silence is one aspect of project management communication that is very seldom utilised. Silence is the language of God, and the use of silence in meetings, project planning sessions, and project negotiations, can be a valuable way to bring in the spiritual dimension. Judi was on a project team at Honeywell that was working on a factory redesign, and the team members agreed that anyone could ask for a moment of silence when needed. Silence was used when there was a high level of disagreement in the room, when a particular problem seemed intractable, or when a situation called for creativity.

CREATIVITY
Recognising that inspiration comes from Spirit, and utilising group spiritual practices from the wisdom traditions to support inspired problem solving

As mentioned in Chapter 2, the word "inspiration" comes from the Latin word "*spirare*," which means spirit, and also means breath. While much of project management is based on linear processes and time lines, there are many opportunities for creativity, especially at the start-up of a project. But creativity is also necessary when risk and uncertainty create unexpected events. Cleden says that:

Creativity should be a core part of the project team's mindset ...
Established wisdom – especially when confronting near-term
uncertainty – can be quite limiting. Creativity offers the chance
to come up with a better solution. (Cleden 2009: 114)

There are many wonderful approaches to encouraging team creativity;
we want to offer here a few explicitly spiritual approaches. The Native
American practice of vision quest and wisdom council were described
in Chapter 2, and these practices can be a very powerful way to tap
into inspiration and creativity.

Another spiritual practice that supports creativity is a team experience
of walking the labyrinth. The labyrinth is a meditative, creativity, and
problem-solving tool that is starting to be used in organisations and
has significant possibilities for providing a non-threatening, non-
religious way to demonstrate the positive use of spiritual practices
in the workplace. The labyrinth is an ancient spiritual ritual common
to cultures as varied as the Native Americans, Norwegians, and
fourteenth-century Catholic monks. It is a form of walking meditation
where one walks on a path marked on the floor or the ground,
beginning on the outside of a circle and gradually working your
way to the center. After some time for reflection in the center, the
walker returns the way he or she came, gradually working one's way
towards the outside of the labyrinth and to the exit (Neal and Miguez
2000).

Joe Miguez facilitated a three-day labyrinth strategic planning
exercise for the top executives of an Italian publishing company. The
leadership team used dialogue methods to develop their list of core
questions about the future of the organisation and then team members
were invited to participate in a reflective walk in the labyrinth while
holding these core questions in their hearts and minds, and being open
to spiritual guidance. The team was able to develop a five-year plan
for the organisation based on the spiritual guidance that team members
received from their labyrinth walks over the three days. This process
has been used for helping teams envision the future, for solving

difficult challenges with a project, and for creative breakthroughs in design and implementation.

Many organisations use games, physical challenges like ropes courses, exercises in the great outdoors like ravine crossings and discovery groups, feedback on strengths and weaknesses, and the arts as a way of helping employees tap into their creativity. Jaworski (1997) established a leadership foundation using the wilderness to help leaders from all walks of life to learn more about themselves and in the process to develop their leadership skills. It included a 24-hour session all alone in the wilderness. Judi has done similar training and vision quest experiences as described in her Edgewalker work. All of these methods work to some degree, but the deepest creativity comes from having a connection to the Great Creator, the Source, God, or whatever you might call the Divine. We believe that it is a great gift to individuals and teams to help them be in touch with their deeper well of creativity.

SUMMARY

We have presented five different approaches to integrating spirituality into project teams, with the goal of helping teams to feel more connected to each other and to their sense of purpose, which leads to greater creativity, innovation, and service to the client.

A spiritual approach to managing project teams can be of benefit to both the organisation and to the team members. There is a long history of leaders taking spiritual approaches to projects, and in more recent times, Project Managers are being more explicit about the implementation of spiritual values and practices. Five approaches were described in this chapter:

1. alignment;
2. spiritual leadership;
3. esprit de corps;
4. communication; and
5. creativity.

Table 6.4 Spiritual approaches to project management teamwork

Approach	Programs	Benefit to Team	Next Steps
Alignment	1. Storytelling 2. Vision quest 3. Nurturing the artist within		
Spiritual Leadership	1. Servant leadership 2. Fry's Spiritual Leadership Survey 3. Spiritual Intelligence Assessment 4. Edgewalker Assessment		
Esprit de Corps	1. Team Spirit Training 2. Customer Service Analysis 3. Belbin's Team Roles		
Communication	1. Bohmian Dialogue 2. Silence		
Creativity	1. Vision quest 2. Wisdom council 3. Labyrinth 4. Outdoor exercises 5. Edgewalker retreat		

Each of these spiritual approaches has been used in project management teams, from small businesses to large organisations such as Pfizer and Xerox. It is our hope that you will feel inspired to adopt one or more of these approaches in your project management team. If you wish to find consultants who can help you adapt any of the processes to your project team, feel free to contact the authors for recommendations of qualified people in your geographic area or your industry.

You may wish to use the grid format in Table 6.4 to select a specific approach or approaches with your team.

CHAPTER 7

THE ORGANISATION AND SPIRITUALITY IN PROJECT MANAGEMENT

In 2003, Providence Health Care (PHC) in Vancouver, Canada, made a major strategic decision to close St Vincent's Arbutus, a 75-bed residential care hospital. The decision to close had been expected for years due to aging infrastructure and no longer being able to meet the needs of residents, yet when it was finally announced people were shocked. As in any major transition, many people experienced the stages of grieving – denial, anger, sadness, depression, and eventually acceptance. The staff had been close-knit and there was a huge sense of loss of community, relationships, and dreams.

PHC is the largest Catholic hospital system in Canada and spiritual values and practices are at the core of who they are and what they do. In a case study they prepared after receiving the 2005 International Spirit at Work Award they wrote:

> *PHC has a strong sense of tradition, compassion, community and spirituality. Our actions are guided by our mission and values, which flow directly from our spiritual base. These values have been embedded in our organisation by the founders and are reinforced by present leaders. For example, PHC has a Vice-President of Mission, Ethics and Spirituality, who is responsible for ethics and diversity services, pastoral care and ensuring the spiritual roots of the organisation are deepened. (Maddix 2005)*

The Providence Health Care Mission states, "Inspired by the healing ministry of Jesus Christ, our staff, physicians and volunteers are dedicated to service and to the support of one another." Their faith tradition enabled them to support one another through difficult times, such as the downsizing of the organisation and the closing of two hospitals. They reported:

> *These events tested people's faith and demonstrated that spirit at work can be found even during the most difficult times. To aid our staff through this transition, PHC's Senior Leadership Team made a commitment to ensure that the process of closing would be in keeping with the mission and core values of the organisation and ensure that employees were treated fairly and with respect. (Maddix 2005)*

The Senior Leadership Team developed a set of Human Resource Principles that were in alignment with the spiritual values of the organisation. These included:

- *Maximize opportunities for staff.*
- *Uphold our values of integrity, stewardship, trust, respect, excellence, and spirituality.*
- *Maintain clear and timely communication with our employees and unions.*
- *Share information and decisions as they become known or clarified.*
- *Provide support and resources for managing change. (Maddix 2005)*

In addition to the normal good human resource practices that are utilised during a downsizing situation, the hospital made an extra commitment to help people deal with the stress of such a large change. They created several channels for open communication with the leadership at tactical and logistical levels as well as emotional and spiritual levels. They also created explicit spiritual practices and ceremonies to help people through the grief, loss, and uncertainty. Here are some specific examples they describe in a case study they wrote for the International Center for Spirit at Work:

> *A meditation room was created for reflection and grief, and there were numerous opportunities for staff to reflect individually and in small groups, to learn from others who were struggling with similar issues and to explore options for new roles. The most significant event at Arbutus was a ceremony of Closure, Thanksgiving and New Beginnings. The Ceremony was given the structure of a spiritual event, a Liturgy. It was filled with prayer, song and ritual. Themes of pain, death, letting go, transition and rebirth were at the heart of the event. These may be Christian themes, but they also resonate with many religions and even humanist beliefs. Candles were lit representing the attributes of compassionate and diligent care, tenacity, gratitude and hope. Seeds from arbutus trees were gathered and distributed to guests as symbols of the Arbutus spirit. Staff was urged to replant these "soul-seeds of compassionate care" in new fields. (Maddix 2005)*

Providence Health Care is an example of a very large organisation that undertook a major systemic change that was in alignment with their core spiritual values and that called forth spiritual leadership. The results of this major transition were positive. Employees felt cared for, respected, and supported. The larger community continued to see Providence Health Care as a significant and valued organisation. And the organisation was able to establish a stronger financial footing and adjust their services to better meet the health needs of the community. But for the organisation, the reason for doing things the way they did were not primarily centered on the bottom line. What was central was that they continued to practice their spiritual values in the closing of the two hospitals, just as they practice those spiritual values in their daily work and their ongoing leadership and decision making.

This chapter examines the macro-system of the organisation and explores its impact on spirituality in project management at this systemic level. The environment, culture, and leadership of the entire company have a big impact on the Project Manager's ability to lead his or her team from a spiritual perspective. We will explore three processes that can be helpful in creating an enlightened organisation where spirituality in project management can thrive. These three processes are:

1. Alignment: aligning vision, meaning, and purpose at the organisational level.
2. Large systems change: using spiritually-based approaches to integrating change in the entire system.
3. Organisational orientations: understanding, measuring and aligning the five organisational orientations.

Let us say at the outset that if you are a Project Manager in an organisation that does not seem to support spirituality in the workplace, do not despair. It is always possible to take a spiritual approach to leading your project management team, regardless of the environment. Your own inner work and commitment to your personal spiritual practices are the most important factors, regardless of the words you use to describe your approach. However, it is much easier and you can go much further along a values-centreed path when the larger organisational system is in alignment with a spiritual approach.

This chapter will not make you an expert on these processes, but it will make you aware of some concepts and tools that can be useful. In case any of these processes intrigue you, we have provided further resources in the footnotes.

ALIGNMENT
Aligning vision, meaning, and purpose at the organisational level

In Chapter 6 we described the steps of creating alignment in teams. Now our focus is on how the organisation creates alignment of vision, meaning, and purpose and how the project management team aligns with the organisation.

The first step in aligning organisational vision, meaning, and purpose is to create shared agreement among organisational stakeholders about this vision, meaning, and purpose. The founder, or founders, of the

Table 7.1 Aligning organisational vision, meaning, and purpose through dialogue with organisation elders

Discussion Questions	Answers from the Elders
What were the original products or services?	
What problem or opportunity did they address?	
Beyond making a profit, what did the founders see as the organisation's contribution to society?	
What stories have you heard about the founder(s) and his or her values?	
Is this founding vision still alive in the organisation?	
What evidence do you have that the founding vision, meaning and purpose are still alive?	
In what ways has the founding vision, meaning and purpose been modified?	
How well is this organisation living in alignment with its current vision?	
What, if anything, would you like to see happen in order to create greater alignment?	

organisation had a very clear sense of the vision when they created the organisation, so it really helps to revisit the founder's reason for starting up the organisation. We recommend inviting the elders of the organisation, the people with the most tenure and organisational memory, to a dialogue about the founding vision, meaning, and purpose of the organisation. We will offer some spirituality processes later in the chapter that help to create alignment with internal and external stakeholders. Above, in Table 7.1, are some questions you can ask of the elders.

You might consider holding this dialogue as a focus group,[1] using a facilitator who is a neutral person, such as an outside consultant who will simply document the conversation and not try to steer it in a particular direction. A good facilitator will make sure to collect multiple points of view and will work with you to interpret the data.

The results of this dialogue can be used to help design some of the large systems change processes described later in this chapter. Or they can be the basis for holding similar focus group sessions in departments throughout the organisation. We have found that discussion of the original vision, meaning, and purpose throughout the organisation helps to reinvigorate and enliven them.

In Chapter 6 we briefly described the use of vision questing in teams. A Xerox plant in Rochester, NY actually sent all their leaders on a week-long spiritual development and ecological leadership retreat that included a 24-hour vision quest in the wilderness with fasting. It took them about a year to involve everyone in this program, and one of the projects that emerged from this experience was the creation of the first completely green and sustainability document center (Ott et al. 1997). This is a wonderful example of integrating good project management processes with spiritual practices and experiences, resulting in a breakthrough project and a new culture for the organisation.

As a Project Manager, it is important for you to create alignment between the vision, meaning, and purpose that you have clarified in the team, and the vision, meaning, and purpose of the organisation. If you are in alignment, it is much easier to find resources and support when you need them. If you are not in alignment, you risk having your project unsupported or even stopped, particularly in economically difficult times.

---

1   For tips on how to run a focus group, go to www-tcall.tamu.edu/orp/orp1.htm

LARGE SYSTEMS CHANGE
Using spiritually-based approaches to integrating change in the entire system

There are two approaches to large systems change that are spiritually based and have been proven to be very effective at changing the culture to a more values-based culture. This values-based culture creates the ideal environment for successful project management because it encourages positive relationships with all stakeholders, supports honesty and authenticity in negotiations instead of politics and unrealistic promises, and encourages the development and implementation of projects that make a positive difference in the world (Pitagorsky 2006). We will discuss each of these briefly. The two approaches are Open Space Technology (OST) and Appreciative Inquiry (AI).

Each approach is designed to include the voices of all of the stakeholders and is focused on building a positive future rather than on being a problem-solving model. The underlying spiritual principle in these models is, "What you pay attention to grows." If you pay attention to what's wrong with the organisation (or departments, customers, vendors, projects), you will continue to notice problems and your energy will be put into solving those problems. Solving problems brings an organisation into a neutral state with regards to its full potential, and does not really help to move it into the future. The approaches described here pay attention to what people are passionate about, what gives them energy, what their dreams and visions are, and what values are central to their lives and mission. Conversations about passion, dreams, gifts, and vision are generative and can help an organisation create what has never existed before. This is a much healthier approach to project management because it allows for greater involvement, creativity, and innovation.

OPEN SPACE TECHNOLOGY

Open Space Technology (OST) was developed by Harrison Owen after a conference he organised where he received feedback that the most interesting and meaningful conversations happened in the breaks. He joked, "What if we designed a conference that was all breaks." The real inspiration for OST actually came from Harrison's work with an African tribe he was with when he was in the Peace Corps. He learned several valuable principles of life that he applied to working with organisations. Four of these principles (and one law) form the guidelines of OST.

1. Whoever comes is the right people.
    This principle reminds people that it is not how many people who come, or even the status of who comes. Rather, what is important is the quality of the interaction and conversation. For good conversation, you need only one other person who shares your passion.

2. Whatever happens is the only thing that could have.
    This principle helps us to remember that real learning and progress only take place when we let go of our own agendas and our original expectations. If everything turned out just the way we expected, life would be dull and unchallenging. We grow from surprises and from learning to handle novelty.

3. Whenever it starts is the right time.
    Creativity and spirit do not punch a time-clock. They appear in their own time, which, by definition, is the right time. They can't be forced. So just because a meeting is scheduled for 2pm, it doesn't mean that creative solutions can be scheduled to emerge. Whenever it starts will be the right time.

4. When it's over, it's over.
    Murphy's Law says that people will stretch out a meeting to fill the allotted time. If two hours have been scheduled for a meeting and the task is completed in 30 minutes, common sense would dictate that it is time to move on. But people seem to feel the need to fulfill the scheduled time. (Harrison 1997)

Each of these principles encourages us to pay attention to energy and to flow with it rather than resist or fight it.

THE ONE LAW

Owen describes the one law as "The Law of Two Feet." He says:

> *... if, during the course of the gathering, any person finds him or herself in a situation where they are neither learning nor contributing, they must use their two feet and go to some more productive place. (Owen 1997: 98)*

There are four major effects of The Law of Two Feet. First, it provides useful feedback to egoists who think they are the only ones with the truth and that it is their God-given duty to impart it to others. If half the room stands up and walks out, it can have a sobering effect.

Second, each participant must take responsibility for the quality of his or her own learning and contribution. There is no planning committee to blame. There are no organisers. If someone chooses to remain in a situation where they are not receiving any benefit, that is their choice.

The third benefit is that The Law of Two Feet creates "bumblebees." As in nature, OST bumblebees are those who flit from location to location, pollinating and cross-pollinating, lending richness and variety to discussions.

The final benefit is the "butterflies." These people often never get involved in any meeting. They may be found at the pool, on the patio, sitting in the bar. At first glance it would seem that butterflies have nothing to contribute. But they are centers of non-action and quiet, and that allows a space for new, unexplored topics to emerge. If you observe butterflies, you may notice that every so often someone will stop by and a significant conversation will emerge.

If you decide to use Open Space Technology as an approach to creating a more spiritual environment in your organisation, it is important to have representatives from all of your key stakeholders in the room. This process can be used for small teams as well as for groups of 3,000 people or more. The designers of the OST retreat will need to have a theme and purpose for the gathering, and a trained facilitator to guide the process. We have seen OST used in sessions as short as two hours, as a part of a larger conference or program, and as much as three days for a large organisational strategic planning session. The process is spiritual because it honors the whole person, is focused on commitment to something greater than ourselves, and allows people to trust their intuition and follow their inner guidance.

Open Space Technology was the process used for a strategic planning session at Yale University Library System. This one day meeting helped individuals to focus on a vision of the future for the library system, guided people to identify what they were passionate about in terms of making the library more effective, and created a structured way for people to look at new ways for the library to live its mission.

While this is not an example of project management, per se, it is an example of a large system using Open Space Technology in a way that creates an environment that is more values-driven, and more supportive of spiritual approaches to project management.

APPRECIATIVE INQUIRY

Organisational leaders are trained and rewarded for focusing on problems and finding ways to fix them. Since we look for problems, those are what we find. By putting our focus on problems, we give them energy and amplify them.

In the mid-1970s, David Cooperrider and his associates at Case Western Reserve University challenged this problem-solving approach and developed the Appreciative Inquiry process (Cooperrider and Whitney 2005). This process suggests that we look for what works well in an organisation rather than what is wrong. In a workshop format, organisational participants are asked a series of questions that provoke stories and descriptions of what works and what the organisation's strengths are. This can be very difficult for people, but once people learn to think this way, there is a major shift in consciousness that opens the way for a much greater sense of meaning and purpose in the major projects that are undertaken by the organisation. This section briefly describes the assumptions of Appreciative Inquiry and provides an overview of a process that can be used with all stakeholders in an organisation.

APPRECIATIVE INQUIRY ASSUMPTIONS

Assumptions are beliefs that are operating at an unconscious level. All groups and organisations operate on assumptions. It becomes the "way we do things here." Shared assumptions allow a group or organisation to operate efficiently because they don't have to constantly stop and determine what they believe or how they should act. However, as the environment changes, the old assumptions may no longer work and should be challenged.

There are eight assumptions of Appreciative Inquiry that make it different from traditional organisational change approaches (Table 7.2).

If you look at these assumptions carefully, you will see that they are very consistent with the core values of most of the world's great

Table 7.2   Assumptions of Appreciative Inquiry

1.	In every society, organisation, or group, something works.
2.	What we focus on becomes our reality.
3.	Reality is created in the moment, and there are multiple realities.
4.	The act of asking questions of an organisation or group influences the group in some way.
5.	People have more confidence and comfort to journey to the future (the unknown) when they carry forward parts of the past (the known).
6.	If we carry parts of the past forward, they should be what is best about the past.
7.	It is important to value differences.
8.	The language we use creates our reality.

spiritual traditions. They emphasise the best of what is possible for individuals and for the collective.

STEPS OF THE PROCESS

The following is a very brief summary of the steps of the Appreciative Inquiry process as described by Sue Hammond, author of *The Thin Book of Appreciative Inquiry*.

One: Choose a Topic

The first step in the Appreciative Inquiry process is to choose a topic for the project team or organisation to study. Appreciative Inquiry is based on asking questions that are appreciative and positive. Some sample questions adapted from Hammond's book for project management are:

- Describe a project when you feel the team or organisation performed really well. What were the circumstances during that time?

- Describe a time when you were proud to be a member of a project team or organisation. Why were you proud?

- What do you value most about being a member of this project team or organisation? Why?

Two: The Interview Process

Once you have determined what the questions are, the next step is to set up an interview process. In a large organisation, the way you do this is to create a design team of employees who are trained in the Appreciative Inquiry process to interview all members, or a significant sample of members of the organisation, using the questions you have chosen.

When people are asked these kinds of questions, it invites them to share stories. This is to be encouraged. Story-telling about things that work in an organisation creates a very positive spiritual energy (Bolman and Deal 1995).

Three: Discovering Themes of Success

After the interview process, the next step is to make sense of all the information that has been gathered. You are looking for common themes of when the project management teams or the entire organisation has performed well. The purpose of this analysis of the interview results is to uncover these themes so that people can know how to do more of what works. This can be done through a brainstorming process or through one of the popular data analysis techniques using post-it notes.

One way to do the analysis is to have the interviewers write themes they heard on flip chart paper posted around the room. Next give people five colored dots that they can place next to the themes that they think are the most important based on what they heard in the interviews and based on their understanding of the organisational culture.

Four: Provocative Propositions

The next step is based on the question of "How can we do more of what works?" The process is one of allowing the stakeholders to begin talking and dreaming about what could be, based on what has already happened. To do this, the design team creates Provocative Propositions.

Provocative Propositions describe an ideal state of circumstances that will foster the climate that creates the possibilities to do more of what works. (Hammond 1998: 32)

While Provocative Propositions are similar to other visioning processes, the major difference is that they are derived from the stories, tradition, and history of the organisation.

To create the Provocative Propositions, find examples of the best stories from the interviews. Review the themes in these stories and the themes that came out of the interviews and determine what circumstances had

Table 7.3   Provocative Propositions from a high-tech project team

Theme	Provocative Propositions
Supportive Environment	• We achieve together • We ask for help and give help when asked • We give credit to others in a timely manner
Open Communication	• We listen first • We give constructive feedback • We value each other's opinions, even when we agree to disagree
Challenge	• We accept challenge as a team, not as individuals • We own the process, and we challenge the process • We challenge each other to learn and tackle new tasks
Teamwork	• We meet our commitments to the team • We take the time to know each other • We have fun and look for the humor in every situation

made the best outcomes possible. Then take the stories and envision what might be. A Provocative Proposition is an affirmative statement that describes the idealised future as if it were already happening. Hammond suggests: "To write the proposition, apply what if to all the common themes. Then write affirmative present-tense statements incorporating the common themes" (Hammond 1998: 32). Table 7.3 lists some examples of Provocative Propositions from a high-tech project team that was having trouble meeting its schedule because of people problems (Brittain 1998).

Five: Experiment with Provocative Propositions

The final step is to identify obstacles and facilitating forces for making the Provocative Propositions a reality. In this step the organisation creates innovation by moving toward the idealised future that it has imagined, based on what is best about the past. Appreciative Inquiry is based on the assumption that organisations, and the people in them, have a natural tendency to move in the direction of images that are the brightest, boldest, and most compelling – that it is possible to move from individual images of possibility and develop collective images of possibility.

SUMMARY OF APPRECIATIVE INQUIRY

This description of Appreciative Inquiry is somewhat general, and we recognise that you could not take what is written here and immediately go into a project team or organisation and create a transformational process based on what has been provided. But we hope it is enough to intrigue you to want to learn more about this process.[2]

The final point is that Appreciative Inquiry is so much more than an organisational development or project management technique. It is a way of being and a way of perceiving the world. As you begin to practice Appreciative Inquiry in life and work you may find a shift in your thinking and actions from one of complaining about a person to appreciating his or her strengths, from feeling victimised by situations to feeling grateful and appreciative for all that you have in life, and from seeing what doesn't work in project management teams and organisations to focusing on what does work. It is a much more enjoyable, effective, and spiritual way of being in the world.

ORGANISATIONAL ORIENTATIONS

A relatively new concept in the field of spirituality in the workplace is Judi Neal's model of Organisational Orientations (Figure 7.1). She

---

2   If you decide you would like to learn more, go to the Taos Institute website and download the article entitled "A positive revolution in change: Appreciative Inquiry." This article provides a case study of work with GTE as well as models, bibliographies, and other resources. If you want to become a skilled facilitator in this methodology, attend one of David Cooperrider's workshops at the Taos Institute. Besides the *Thin Book of Appreciative Inquiry*, you may also wish to read *Lessons From the Field: Applying Appreciative Inquiry*, edited by Sue Hammond and Cathy Royal. This book is out of print but may be found in libraries. It is full of detailed case studies and very detailed information.

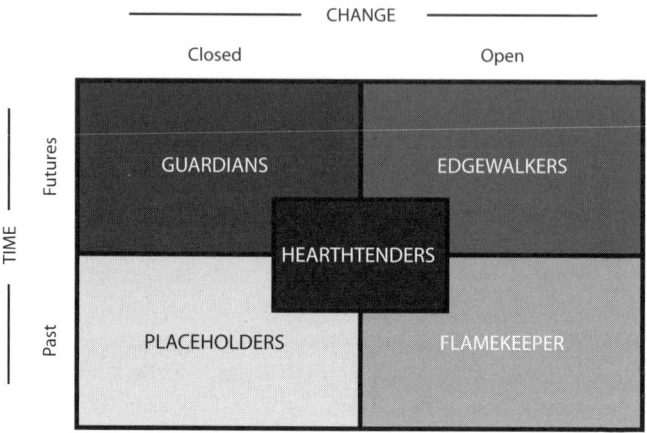

Figure 7.1   Organisational orientation model

studied leaders who had a strong commitment to their own spiritual life and who were also pioneers in their field. These leaders are called "Edgewalkers" because they build bridges between the spiritual world and the world of business.

Edgewalkers are just one of the five organisational orientations she found in her research. The other four are Flamekeepers, Hearthtenders, Placeholders, and Guardians (Neal 2006). Every human being has some aspects of each of these Organisational Orientations, as does every project management team and every organisation. These orientations are based on two factors:

1. *Relationship to Time*; and
2. *Relationship to Change*.

The *Relationship to Time* factor is a continuum between focus on the past and focus on the future. The *Relationship to Change* factor is a continuum between being closed to change and being open to change.

Each of these orientations can change depending on one's situation, although we all have a preferred way of looking at and interacting with the world. The table on the following page (Table 7.4) provides a brief definition of each of the orientations and their application to an organisational culture that supports spirituality and project management.

Neal has developed an Organisational Orientation Survey that helps individuals to understand their personal profile of these five orientations. Each of us is sometimes an Edgewalker, a Hearthtender, a Flamekeeper, a Placeholder, and a Guardian. And each of us is more comfortable in one of these worldviews rather than the others. It helps to know and understand one's profile and to learn about the strengths that your orientation brings to the project and to the organisation. The Organisational Orientations Survey also creates a team and organisational profile and provides feedback on employee perceptions of whether the organisation is an Edgewalker Organisation, a Hearthtender Organisation, a Flamekeeper Organisation, a Placeholder Organisation, or a Guardian Organisation.

The ideal mix for project management is to have an organisation with a balance of Edgewalkers, Hearthtenders, and Guardians. Edgewalkers bring the creative thinking, the spiritual centeredness, and an ability to envision the future. Hearthtenders bring the ability to manage the day-to-day details and make sure that nothing slips through the cracks. Guardians bring the gift for anticipating what could go wrong and a focus on helping to prevent problems.[3]

The form at the end of this chapter (Table 7.5) can be used to assess your project team profile on the five orientations.

---

3   For more information, visit http://www.edgewalker.org

Table 7.4   Five organisational orientations and their application to project management

Organisational Orientation	Definition	Application to Project Management
Edgewalkers	Edgewalkers are people who walk between worlds and have the ability to build bridges between different worlds. They have a strong spiritual life and are very grounded and effective in the everyday material world.	Edgewalkers are excellent at communicating with different project stakeholders. They are also the visionaries who understand the purpose and meaning of a project and can communicate that to others. In addition, they are likely to be the risk-takers when things are uncertain.
Hearthtenders	Hearthtenders are the people who do the day-to-day work of the organisation and who are focused on serving others.	Hearthtenders manage the multiple details of a project, tracking action items, gating factors and milestones. They are also committed to creating a sense of 'family' in the team or organisation.
Flamekeepers	Flamekeepers are those people who keep the original vision and values of the project and organisation alive.	Flamekeepers are the ones who remind the rest of the project team or organisation about the meaning and purpose of the project and about the values that they have agreed to live by in their work together.

Table 7.4   Continued

Organisational Orientation	Definition	Application to Project Management
Placeholders	Placeholders provide stability and predictability to the organisation. They are the keepers of the boundaries and can keep a project or organisation from going over the edge. They tend to resist change for the sake of change and are comfortable with routine.	Placeholders provide a balance to others (especially Edgewalkers) who may want to take too many risks. They question suggested changes to the project, and can be seen as blocking progress, but they usually have the best interests of the project in mind, if you can listen to the kernel of truth that they are trying to express.
Guardians	Guardians have a gift for analyzing and/or sensing what could go wrong before it happens. They are committed to protecting people and the organisation from potential harm.	Guardians in a project are the ones who look for potential problems with actions the team might be planning. They are excellent at analysing project plans and seeing tasks, deadlines, and other activities could potentially pose a problem for project success.

Table 7.5   Project team organisational orientation analysis

Organisational Orientations	Our strengths in this domain (Example: people, policies, training, culture)	Our weakness in this domain (Example: people, policies, training, culture)	Action steps we can take (Example: hiring, training, assessment, coaching)
Edgewalkers			
Hearthtenders			
Flamekeepers			
Placeholders			
Guardians			

SUMMARY

In this chapter we have looked at the organisational level of spirituality in the workplace and discussed the role that the corporate culture can play in supporting spirituality in project management. We suggested three processes that help to create an organisational environment for spirituality in project management. They are:

1. aligning vision, meaning, and purpose of the project with the vision, meaning, and purpose of the organisation;
2. using spiritually-based approaches to integrating change in the organisation such as Open Systems Technology and Appreciative Inquiry; and
3. understanding, measuring, and aligning the five organisational orientations in a way that embraces spirituality in project management.

In the next chapter we discuss the role of spirituality and project management at the global level, and explore the role that the field of project management can take in helping to solve major problems facing humanity and the planet.

CHAPTER 8

THE PLANET AND SPIRITUALITY IN PROJECT MANAGEMENT

In this chapter we consider global issues and where spirituality in project management can contribute. We consider the sustainability of the Earth with its growing and ever demanding population, climate change, and shrinking natural resources. We look at the need for global scale projects to deal with these concerns.

Many are concerned about the sustainability of the planet with the huge population growth – seven billion now and forecast to grow to nine billion by 2020. Will we be able to feed all these people, house them, clothe them, provide sufficient clean water, and – also very important – find meaningful work that enables them to grow in body, mind, emotion and spirit?

We know we have been overworking our planet. We have taken many of the natural resources and used them up for energy and failed to replace them or sustain them. For example, as we reduce our dependence on petroleum products for energy, we have turned to bio-fuels. While this helps the environment, it has driven the costs of food very high, affecting the nutritional health of many people who live on the margins.

We have, however, also become much more aware of our impact on the world and, we hope, more cautious about our part in it.

In 2010, a British Petroleum (BP) sub-sea pipeline ruptured in the Gulf of Mexico, threatening untold long-term damage to the local ecology, and this shortly after the devastation created there by Hurricane

Katrina. BP said that their offshore drilling platform had another three fail-safe devices to prevent the leak of oil into the sea before the explosion that led to the leak, but all three appeared to have failed. The main talk at a project management conference in China recently was the re-directing of three major rivers northward to satisfy the need for water in major expanding cities. Similarly, in South Africa the Orange Free River has been dammed and diverted north to provide water for Johannesburg and Pretoria. Do we really know what the environmental impact will be of such major changes to the local environment and its impact on water courses and climate? Most parts of the world now call for every relevant project to have an Environmental Impact Study and Statement on projects such as these so that these matters receive full consideration before projects go ahead. But are these powerful enough to lead mankind to do the right thing? Will they go far enough to protect future generations? Or are they just another check mark on the project management 'to do' list?

Severe weather, earthquakes, and tsunamis have caused unprecedented damage to human communities, with major loss of life. In 2010 Lloyds of London, the insurers, had their largest set of claims for natural disasters ever! We cannot control Mother Nature, but we can learn to be much more respectful and in harmony with her. In 2011 we experienced the worst earthquake and tsunami ever in Japan with critical damage to a nuclear power plant, a dreadful earthquake in Christchurch, New Zealand, and yet another in Chile. We wonder why, and ponder whether we have any way of dealing with these "naturally" occurring events or are they just literally "acts of God." Al Gore (2006), in his documentary *An Inconvenient Truth*, provided a great deal of evidence that humankind is causing climate change, and he predicted that the frequency of severe weather events and earthquakes would increase.

After the March 25, 2011 earthquake and tsunami in Japan, and the resultant crisis at the Fukushima Daiichi nuclear plant, the public learned that the tsunami emergency plan was only one-page long. Historically, there had been earthquakes and tsunamis in that area of the same magnitude as the 2011 earthquake, but plant project planners had only looked back at the last 150 years or so. If they had been more in touch with the larger patterns of earthquakes in that geographic area, they would have realised that a similar earthquake and tsunami tended to hit that area every thousand years or so and was quite overdue. A more spiritual perspective on project planning takes a long-term view, with a commitment to caring for the entire planet and for future generations, rather than focusing on short-term gain for a few.

The Celtic Christian tradition, and many other religious traditions, believe all work is sacred, however small or humble. For example, one can find Celtic prayers for cleaning the hearth stone. Mother Teresa said, "Not all of us can do great things. But we can do small things with great love." Whether we believe that all work is sacred or not, it is certainly true that most human projects are for the benefit of mankind, or at least were conceived that way. In this sense they represent spiritual work. But do they? Some may be ill conceived, and there are increasing calls for new projects that would help the world environmentally by cleaning the atmosphere and water sources on earth, and for sustainability projects to ensure that the world's natural resources are used more sparingly and fairly. We need greater attention to possible side effects such as oil or nuclear disasters with their horrific impact on the earth or sea and its creatures including us!

Today a key need is to put the "public" back into public relations. This means keeping people well informed, not just with good news but also with bad news. When things go wrong, people want to know what is happening and how it affects them, what is being done to improve the situation and how long it is likely to take – even if it is going to take a long time. The public hates being kept in the dark or hearing bad news that comes too late to take alternative actions.

In our time project management has moved from an attitude of "stand back, we know what we are doing and will hand over the output of the project at the end," to a more consultative approach, talking with the owner of the project and agreeing the scope and plan for the project. Now we focus on agreeing the whole project with its owner, carrying out an Environmental Impact Study and ameliorating any downsides and in the extreme cancelling the project. We routinely now also consult with all the stakeholders in the project and endeavor to manage the majority's concerns. In Canada, when they discovered that land taken from the First Peoples had not been bought as freehold but was on a 99-year lease, a consensus approach to the construction of hydro-electric power schemes was initiated. As we can imagine this is perhaps the hardest type of stakeholder management yet in the world and might well be a sign of things to come. Certainly a race that always desired a sustainable world (see Chapter 1 quotation) would be unlikely to want to commit to projects that they saw as "harming" the world we live in. The environmental protections that they demand might make many projects unviable.

Project Management will become more complex with the need for consensus and collective wisdom of all stakeholders. The project leadership skills in EQ and SQ will become even more important in facilitating the utilisation of collective wisdom.

> *Collective Wisdom refers to knowledge and insight gained through group and community interaction. At a deeper level, however, it is about our living connection to each other and the living interdependence we share in our neighborhoods, organizations and world community. (Briskin et al. 2009: xiii)*

Briskin et al. continue:

> *When we join together the terms collective and wisdom, we reach a whole new synthesis of insight and revelation ... the collective eye can pick up patterns of order, variation, and connections; wisdom can detect meaning and human values that arise spontaneously from a particular situation. We achieve, to paraphrase the words of the psychiatrist Viktor Frankl, an ability to weave together the slender threads of a fractured whole into a firmer pattern of meaning. To share collective wisdom with others is to make meaning from disparate threads and weave together a fresh understanding. (Briskin et al. 2009: 8)*

We can see this in the things that have happened in our lifetimes that we thought impossible: the end of racial tensions in the American deep South; the end of the Northern Ireland troubles; the end of Apartheid in South Africa; the collapse of the Berlin Wall and Iron Curtain; and all that they stood for. We are living in a world where human consciousness is growing and with it the acceptance of our interconnectedness. This brings the need for a fresh and new approach to managing intra-planetary projects:

> *Real change comes from an awareness of our deep connectedness. For some this may mean a spiritual awakening, a transformation that begins with the human heart. For others, it may be a more intellectual process, coming to see anew the need for addressing an emerging environmental ethic and related social issues involving business, health, education, and the disparity of wealth within and between nations. (Briskin et al. 2009: 9)*

Wilkinson and Pickett (2011) demonstrate through published statistics that a smaller gap between rich and poor leads to a better quality of life and vice versa.

Certain kinds of conversations and collective endeavors lead us to the wisdom we possess in groups that is unavailable to us as individuals. Wheatley envisions:

> *A world which constantly surprises us with the wisdom that exists not in any one of us, but in all of us. And a world where we learn that the wisdom we need to solve our problems is available when we talk together. (Wheatley 2005)*

There is a good scientific explanation for this, because this is how all life works. As separate ideas or entities become connected to each other, life surprises us with emergence – the sudden appearance of new capacity and intelligence. All living systems work in this way. We humans became confused and lost sight of this remarkable process by which individual actions, when connected, lead to much greater capacity.

All this points to the need to forge a collective vision for each global project that delivers total meaning and purpose to all the participants. The vision needs to align with them all. This usually requires an iterative process that starts with a draft vision that is shared and improved upon through conversation and reflection by all the stakeholders, including someone who is a voice for the environment and someone who is a voice for the future. When it comes to stakeholders we need those who can really represent the future. As the Dalai Lama has said, and as Native Americans have been saying for a long time, we need to ensure that whatever we make or do does not adversely affect the next seven generations.

The world is drawing together with more and more connectedness. We wait to see with great interest if this will be true for the world's religions sharing more and more of their values while beginning to explore their differences through interfaith dialogue. They have much further to go in seeking a common spirituality in this world, but it is eminently worth doing.

As modern communication methods continue to develop and bring us the possibility to communicate by word (text, internet, and e-mail), orally through telephonics (mobiles, radio, and landlines), and through pictures and film (internet and phone) the ability to interconnect instantly and converse deeply is growing all the time. This has enabled many world projects to operate 24/7 by means of the project work encircling the world with virtual global teams.

In Alan's APM group they are working with an Australian Company called Change Track Pty, from Sydney. They have a tool for program and project managers to invite individual group members representing stakeholder groups to go online and answer 24 questions. Each group can have up to ten members. The answers are compared with a database of 500,000 sets of data on change initiatives and programs and projects, and the program or project manager is offered a 3D profile map showing where the stakeholder groups are in terms of the final desired outcome and how to get the program or project home to where it is desired. This product enables stakeholders to be looked at individually and in groups to see where they are against the question set and how they or the project needs to change to achieve a mutually satisfactory outcome. This product is presently only available through APM Group's Accredited Consulting Organisations (see www.apmg-international.com).

There is a problem sometimes with getting a stakeholder group that is external to the organisation to use an online product. We may have to take the technology to some of these groups to enable them to take part. This is particularly true of some lobby groups on public projects where they may not have access to computers and the internet. Some of these projects may have to set up local internet cafes or other venues such as local public libraries where they can install the technology for local users who do not have ready access to computers. These may need to be manned for some of the time so that those who are illiterate or too young or too old to understand can be helped. The helpers need to be sensitive so as not to lead the stakeholders in answering the questions. This is particularly true if they are youngsters, elderly, or other vulnerable people.

Another problem is to find people in groups who can represent future generations. One set of people to turn to could be "futurists," from groups such as The Foresight Network (see http://shapingtomorrowmain. ning.com/?xg_source=msg_mes_network), Edgewalkers (see www. edgewalkers.org), Insights (see www.getei.com/insights.html), and Shaping Tomorrow (see www.shapingtomorrow.com) to ask them if they have a facility to answer for future stakeholders.

Another strategy (not mutually exclusive to the futurists) is to invite young people, children, and adolescents, to take part, but this will need care to make sure they are neither manipulated and in many cultures not put at risk. In some cultures it would be inappropriate for a male questioner to put questions to groups of or single women (for example – Islam). In some cultures if adults are working with young people the questioners will need to have been checked and cleared from any kind of record regarding inappropriate behavior with young people. In the UK this is called Criminal Record Bureau or CRB check. These include criminal records where people have been taken to court and found guilty but also where they have received a police caution instead and no record.

The Native Americans have Shamans or holy men, who walk the future often using extreme heat and/or drugs to induce semi-hypnotic states. The Biblical prophets were called to be prophetically pointing to future outcomes if society and mankind continue with certain behaviors. "Repent" means to turn away from a direction that is leading to a negative outcome and to turn towards a direction that is good for humanity. Perhaps a Shaman or Prophet or equivalent from other faiths could help Project Managers in discerning the future. Michael Rennie, a change management consultant with McKinsey in Australia, did just this. He brought Gita Bellin, a local shaman, into the company to do spiritual work with clients on change management projects – with measurable success. There are people who now serve professionally as "corporate shamans" (Blumenfeld 2008, Whiteley 2002).

Project Managers could create groups to represent future generations asking them to role play around the scenario, not so different to the scenario planning ideas that Shell used to train their future managers and that Joseph Jaworski (1997) used when he worked there.

The groups could be created as in the Native American's Wisdom Council process where depending where individuals sat in the round, they represented different age groups such as North = Children, South = Adolescents, East = Adults, and West = Future Generations.

Project Managers could invite faith leaders to participate to brainstorm potential outcomes of programs and projects on society, particularly spiritually positive and negative ones.

Another possibility is to use the World Cafe model where small groups (six to ten people in each) are created at random and asked to look at a particular discussion question. After five to ten minutes the groups are asked to regroup with one or two remaining in each group to explain what the previous group had discussed, the rest moving on to a new group. After a few rounds each group is asked to say what that group discussed and to describe its key findings.

Another model is to use Open Space Technology, which is a simple way to run productive meetings, for five to 2,000 plus people, and a powerful way to lead any kind of organisation, in everyday practice and extraordinary change (see www.openspaceworld.org). This methodology was discussed in Chapter 7 as an organisational approach, but is also very useful for global scale projects with multiple stakeholders.

The possibilities for the world and the human race seem greater than ever. If the Project and Program Managers of the future develop their Emotional and Spiritual Intelligence as much as they can, and recognise the interconnectedness of their teams and stakeholders, the possibilities seem endless for creating major global projects to feed mankind; to provide clean water and sanitation; to use energy wisely; to invent and develop new power sources and new ways to travel; to act sustainably; to clean up our ozone layer; and to settle down the climate. This blue planet could become a real haven for mankind of the future to live in peace and love with each other and run fantastical projects for their fellow citizens that really deliver the outputs which we all crave.

CHAPTER 9

THE HISTORY AND THE FUTURE OF PROJECT MANAGEMENT

We recognise that projects have been undertaken by mankind from the start of civilisation over 5,000 years ago. Modern project management began with military projects in the Second World War. Since then the science of project management (as it began then) has developed into a science and art. We believe it has the potential to develop into a spiritual practice as well. This chapter will provide a brief overview of the evolution of Project Management through the present time and our vision of Project Management in the future (Figure 9.1).

Modern civilian project management post-war began with network planning and the use of a method called the critical path method

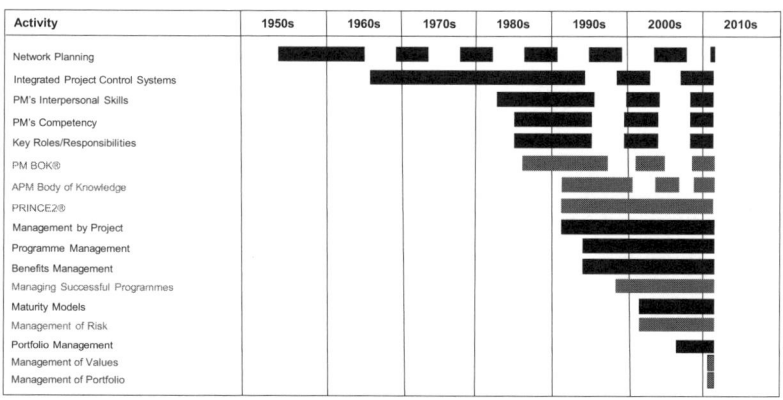

Activity	1950s	1960s	1970s	1980s	1990s	2000s	2010s
Network Planning							
Integrated Project Control Systems							
PM's Interpersonal Skills							
PM's Competency							
Key Roles/Responsibilities							
PM BOK®							
APM Body of Knowledge							
PRINCE2®							
Management by Project							
Programme Management							
Benefits Management							
Managing Successful Programmes							
Maturity Models							
Management of Risk							
Portfolio Management							
Management of Values							
Management of Portfolio							

Key: Grey indicates proprietary products; Black indicates generic subject

Figure 9.1   Abbreviated recent history of PPPM

(CPM) in the mid-1950s. DuPont, the chemical company, developed CPM, which used logic and time estimates for activities to determine the longest path of activities through a logic network and hence the shortest duration for the delivery of the project outputs. At about the same time the US Department of Defense developed a more sophisticated method called PERT – Program Evaluation and Review Technique – which basically did the same thing but with probabilities attached to individual activity durations. The whole focus of project management was to deliver outputs on time.

In the 1960s the driver for project management was to invent a fully integrated project management control system computer tool (mainframe). These were huge programs designed to enable all the details of each of an organisation's projects to be fed into the system at the definition stage, and monitoring data to be captured in progress, in the hope that the organisation would know the situation on each and every one of its projects. The hardest part is to convince the project management staff to feed in the data, because in most cases the tool is then used to police their progress and beat them up if it is lagging. People are still trying to develop such systems but with much the same problems.

In the early 1980s the demand was for people who could project manage people over whom they had no direct control. Companies bought large computer systems but this approach, with its focus on time and cost, appeared to have changed nothing in terms of successful project outputs.

So began the quest for courses and interventions that could help Project Managers develop and grow their interpersonal skills including communications, delegation and inspiration, monitoring progress, resolving conflicts, and demonstrating personal competence. Shortly afterwards, academics and others started to develop lists of competencies necessary for good project management and Project Managers. This might be considered as the first step in looking to Emotional Intelligence competencies as being helpful.

At the end of the 1980s, the Project Management Institute of America developed its first Body of Knowledge on project management. This was shortly followed in the early 1990s by the Association for Project Management's (APM) Body of Knowledge, thought by many to be a list of competences, and then shortly afterwards the International Project Management Association's (IPMA) International Competence Baseline (ICB). All three documents have been revised and updated a number of times. Also in the early 1990s the UK government paid to have computer project management methodology converted into one suitable for government projects. Initially called PRINCE, the PRINCE2 version was altered so it could be used generically on any project.

During that time, an Austrian School from Vienna introduced the idea of Management by Projects, which opened the realm of project management into many other areas as a way of managing all business changes in organisations.

The 1990s also saw the advent of Program Management, the idea of running a set of projects with a common strategic goal as a program. This led to the concept of Benefits Management. This is the idea that we do projects to deliver benefits to organisations and introduced the notion of Business Change Managers to take the project outputs and convert them into a set of business benefits, or the desired organisational outcome. The Office of Government Commerce (OGC) in the UK (now re-branded as part of the Cabinet Office) produced a new *Managing Successful Programmes* guide for government.

In the 2000s Maturity Models for project management came into being and then later a real focus on Portfolio Management – the management of an organisation's whole change portfolio of programs and projects. OGC also published its guide to the *Management of Risk* and more recently its Maturity Model P3M3®. This was followed by OGC guides on *Management of Value and Management of Portfolio*.

There is presently a great interest in the management of what are being called Complex Projects and as you will have seen in this book, much of its focus is on the higher competencies of emotional and spiritual competences (EQ and SQ).

For the future we expect organisational and systems change to be a continuing phenomena, and for the management of change to take prime importance over "business as usual," in terms of senior management effort. The best way to deliver change is more and more being seen as through Portfolio, Program and Project Management (PPPM). More people are being asked during their formation to run a project or program as a learning and development exercise. More career structures for those wishing to focus on a career in PPPM are appearing, and such career paths are being seen as increasingly important.

For those just beginning their careers, the tools offered by PMI and IPMA's members are excellent and those requiring a method to manage their programs and projects will find MoP, MSP, PRINCE2, and P3O from the OGC stable a great help.

As these careers move forward into mega, complex projects, the future forecasts the need for competent PPMs to develop their Emotional Intelligence and Spiritual Intelligence skills. We believe this book, with its emphasis on the spirituality of Project Management, can help in many ways. So let's take a look at our vision of the future of Project Management and the important role that spirituality has to play in the evolution of this field.

THE FUTURE OF THE SPIRITUALITY OF PROJECT MANAGEMENT

Project Management is impacted by the prevailing business philosophy that puts total emphasis on the bottom line, often to the detriment of many stakeholders. Big business (as well as big government, big banks, and large religious organisations) tend to want to preserve stability and preserve their power base. Stability is a valuable thing, but in recent times, we have seen the limits of some of our current systems. The economy has imploded, political groups have become more polarised, the environment is suffering from rapid and unhealthy climate change, and conflicts are erupting in areas where peoples have been oppressed for a generation or more. Business has seen itself as detached from these world problems.

At the same time, low-paid workers, emerging markets, and the hunger for resources are often connected in some way to these global issues. What if business were to start to see itself as part of the solution, rather than trying to defend itself from claims that it is part of the problem? Project Management, by its nature, is disruptive to current stability through the introduction of something new; a new building or highway, a new technology; or new way of doing marketing for example. A spiritual approach to the introduction of the change is more likely to be adopted and implemented smoothly. This spiritual approach must focus on meaning and purpose for all involved, and it must focus on more than just the bottom line.

In the future, as spirituality in organisations becomes a more central part of the paradigm, we expect to see a real shift in the way projects are managed. In the past ten years or so, enlightened organisations have started to adopt new management concepts like the triple bottom line (Bowden, Lane, and Martin 2001, Fry 2012), sustainability (Hawken 2010), values-centered organisations (Barrett 2006), and spiritual intelligence (Wigglesworth 2010, Zohar and Marshall 2000). Aburdene (2010) captures the shift in business consciousness very well in her book *Megatrends 2010: The Rise of Conscious Capitalism.*

As human beings grow in their moral and spiritual development, they evolve from an ego-centric worldview to a global-centric worldview. Leading-edge organisations are developing in a similar fashion from a profit-centric worldview to a global-centric worldview with a commitment to balancing the needs of multiple stakeholders, including the stakeholders in the future, as discussed in Chapter 8. Because Project Management is affected by the prevailing worldview of business, we expect to see an increasing emphasis on values-centered and spiritual ways of planning and implementing projects.

Our vision of the future is one where projects are designed with a commitment to sustainability, social justice, team spiritual development, community development, respect and dignity for all stakeholders, and a commitment to making the world a better place, above and beyond profit. The problems of the world are getting larger and more complex. A spirituality of Project Management can provide new ways to tackle these challenges with confidence.

As we look ahead to the future, we can foresee the following possibilities for spirituality in Project Management at the four levels described in this book: self, team, organisation, and planet. We allow ourselves to envision a positive future for each of these levels in this next section.

THE FUTURE OF PROJECT MANAGEMENT AND THE SELF

All change begins with the self. We foresee that in the future the Project Manager will begin a new project with a time of deep personal self-reflection about the project and how it fits in with his or her values and sense of calling. The Project Manager may hire a spiritual coach or workplace chaplain to help the individuals on the team to integrate their own spirituality with the work of the project. Each person would take some kind of spiritual assessment such as the Spiritual Intelligence Survey (Wigglesworth 2010) or the Edgewalker Profile (Neal 2011). They will also agree to adopt or deepen some kind of contemplative practice, such as prayer, meditation, yoga, or journaling. People would be hired based on technical competence, emotional intelligence, and spiritual intelligence.

The project overview debrief would include all the traditional information such as design, milestones, resources, relationships with stakeholders, costs, and completion goals. But it would also include information on the spiritual purpose of the project, and what it means to the PM in his or her own spiritual journey. Each individual on the team would be invited to share the spiritual meaning of the project with the rest of the team members.

The result of a project team that pays attention to the integration of spirituality and the work of project management is individuals who are motivated and inspired and use more of their discretionary energy to help the project to succeed. Turnover is reduced, because individuals want to be a part of something bigger than themselves. Stress levels are lower in a team that hires for spiritual intelligence, resulting in less absenteeism or on-the-job absenteeism. A greater level of synergy can occur when the Project Manager consciously works to integrate spirituality at the level of the team.

THE FUTURE OF PROJECT MANAGEMENT AND THE TEAM

In the future, new projects will begin with a retreat of all the team members, ideally in a setting that is beautiful and connected to nature. The PM and the spiritual coach or workplace chaplain will have designed an experience that helps the team members to get to know one another in terms of their experience, their expertise, their vision for the project, and how this project fits into each person's spiritual journey. Chapter 5 provides some specific exercises that can be used on this retreat. Ground rules are set to encourage open dialogue about faith and spirituality in a climate of freedom, with no proselytising. Team members will be taught methods of deep listening, such as Bohmian dialogue, and will receive Team Spirit training, such as that described by Barry Heermann (1997). The Project Manager talks about how each team has a unique team soul and a unique spiritual calling. The team of the future will participate in spiritual exercises, such as a vision quest, that can help the team to be in touch with the soul of the project and with this team's unique calling.

The team of the future, like any present day team, will develop the project plan, with milestones and deliverables. However, in addition, the project plan includes periodic times when the team comes together to renew spiritual energy and to revitalise the vision of the project. The emphasis in the team switches from focusing only on deadlines and deliverables to a more holistic view that incorporates the development of each team member and the team as a whole, and a focus on stakeholder relationships. The team may use spiritual practices such as prayer, visualisation, affirmations, and intuition to help guide them through the inevitable difficult times.

Upon completion of the project, the team will come together in a retreat one final time to review their work together and to reflect on the meaning and purpose of the project, its role in each person's life, and how it will make a positive difference in the world. The Project Manager may work with the spiritual coach for the team to devise a closing ritual that pulls the task, the relationships, and the spiritual meaning all together for the team.

Teams that work with a conscious attention to the spiritual aspect of a project will be more likely to bring a project in on time and within budget. They will be able to work through conflicts and different points of view in a healthy way that leads to higher respect and trust in a team. This higher trust-level, in turn, leads to less internal need for control and accountability, because each team member knows that he or she can rely on others to keep their commitments.

THE FUTURE OF PROJECT MANAGEMENT AND THE ORGANISATION

We think it is essential for the sake of society, social justice, and sustainability, that organisations integrate spiritual values and practices into their culture, and support the integration of spirituality and Project Management. Spiritual organisations, just like spiritual individuals, have a commitment to something greater than themselves. They have a sense of meaning and purpose that is beyond just making a profit. They want to make a positive difference.

In the future, the spiritual organisation will be open about its spiritual purpose in the world and will have formal ways of reflecting periodically on its values and practices. As projects are proposed and undertaken, they will be evaluated on whether they fit with those spiritual mission and values. Top leaders will be accountable for the spiritual support they provide to Project Managers, Program Managers and project teams. Top leaders will also be called upon to remind the organisation of its larger purpose, and to assess the impact of major projects on an expanded set of stakeholders. Their focus will be on the client, as it should be, but will also include the employees, the communities, the indigenous people, and the land. In addition, their focus will be on future generations.

Top leadership will assess policies and procedures of the organisation against their core spiritual values. They will conduct a spiritual values-audit, such as that developed by Richard Barrett (2006), and modify plans and actions to ensure the organisation is in alignment with its core values. These values will include a deep respect for the uniqueness and spirit of each individual and a commitment to their spiritual development. Leaders will model this through their personal commitment to their own faith or spiritual tradition and will be open about their spirituality, while being careful not to pressure others to believe as they do. The organisation will be a safe place for people to bring their whole selves to work and where they are encouraged to be authentic and transparent.

This kind of organisation is values-centered and built on trust, which means it will be a lot less bureaucratic. You do not need to have a lot of controls in place when people are trusting and trustworthy. Less bureaucracy means more flexibility and freedom, allowing the organisation to respond quickly and innovatively to change. People love to work in an environment like this, and a spiritually centered organisation can attract and retain the highest talent. All other things being equal, clients would be more likely to want to work with this kind of an organisation, because of their great reputation and strong social capital.

THE FUTURE OF SPIRITUALITY AND THE PLANET

We are living in a time when it is crucial for all of us to become more aware of what the human race is doing to the planet, and for each of us to take action to have a more positive impact in whatever way we can. Recently Judi was having lunch with a colleague who is very environmentally active. This colleague told her that if everyone cut their meat consumption in half, it would have a greater positive impact on the environment than if everyone cut their driving in half. Eating less meat seems so much more doable than cutting one's driving by half.

There is a corollary for Project Management. There are projects out there that will be very feasible and cost effective and will have a significant benefit to the planet. In the future, we will need the best and brightest Project Managers to work on these kinds of projects. Project Managers will have worked on their own consciousness and self-awareness enough to realise how interconnected we are to each other, and how interconnected our living systems are.

Project Managers will deal with questions such as how we reduce our dependence on fossil fuels and collectively and effectively turn to more renewable forms of energy. They will work on problems of world hunger and effective food distribution systems. They will work on economic development issues leading to better education and support for underdeveloped areas, and improved quality of life for those affected by war and strife. Many large planetary issues need to be addressed with the skills and competencies of Project Managers and from a high level of spiritual intelligence. Otherwise there is the danger that projects will be undertaken only for personal gain, and the work could be suboptimal and perhaps even cause harm to stakeholders who are disempowered.

Ironically, the future of Project Management entails drawing on ancient wisdom of all of the world's religious and spiritual traditions, which have preserved the wisdom of what works for the greatest good.[1]

---

1   In November 2012, the Tyson Center for Faith and Spirituality in the Workplace hosted a conference called "Wisdom at Work" to explore the ways in which ancient and modern religious traditions can provide guidance to challenges and opportunities in organisations.

SUMMARY

Project management has its roots in the earliest major projects created in service of human spirituality, such as the pyramids, the Great Wall of China, and the Taj Mahal. Over the centuries, as rational thinking took predominance, the connection between spirituality and project management was lost. Human rationality and scientific thinking have made great contributions to the development of civilisation and to the quality of life for many of the peoples on this earth. It was evolutionary to move out of the superstitious thinking of primitive religions (Wilber 2001). However, now we have arrived at a place where we are out of balance, and have lost many of the positive aspects of spirituality.

We hope we have made that connection much more explicit in this book as we discussed the emergence of the field of faith and spirituality in the workplace and explained the relevance of spirituality to project management. This book described several of the virtues that can guide project managers in their work with project owners, project investors, team members, and other key stakeholders. We suggest that taking a values-centered approach to project management, while difficult in today's highly competitive environment, is the approach that is most likely to have positive outcomes.

Throughout this book we have discussed the four levels at which a spiritual approach to project management can be implemented. They are individual, team, organisation, and planetary. In Part II of this book we offered theories, case examples, and practical suggestions for actions the Project Manager can take to explicitly integrate spirituality in the project team. Spirituality is an essential aspect of our humanness, but generally lies dormant in most project teams. It is our hope that the ideas and information provided in this book can help you to make the implicit more explicit. There are many more resources available than the ones provided in these chapters, but you can at least get started with what is here.

The first level of integrating spirituality and project management is the level of the individual self, and the primary focus at this level is the development of self-awareness and a commitment to personal, professional, and spiritual growth. At this level, one of the major roles of the project manager is creating a clear understanding of the meaning and purpose of the project in a way that aligns with each individual team member's virtues and values. Project management is a valuable opportunity for Project Managers to develop their team members as whole human beings, encompassing body, mind, emotion, and spirit.

The second level is the team level. This book offers five ways to integrate spirituality and project management at the project team level:

1. Alignment: aligning vision, meaning, and purpose at the team level.
2. Spiritual leadership: seeing oneself as a Servant Leader to the team and being committed to helping each team member be a Servant Leader to others.
3. Esprit de corps: understanding and honoring the collective spirit of the team.
4. Communication: using non-traditional communication methods as a way of building trust and openness.
5. Creativity: recognising that inspiration comes from Spirit, and utilising group spiritual practices from the wisdom traditions to support inspired problem solving.

In our experience, the individual and team levels are the best places to begin the integration of spirituality and project management. In a healthy organisation or project, the kind of approaches and exercises we describe are natural outgrowths of the development approaches that have gone before. We would not recommend any of these approaches in a project team that was filled with high levels of unhealthy conflict, high degrees of apathy, or very strong resistance to change. These are symptoms of something deeper in a project team that will need to be addressed before attempting the more sophisticated and mature approaches of spirituality and project management.

The third level is the organisational or systemic level. Every project is embedded in a much larger system, whether it is a company, a consortium of companies, a government, or a non-governmental organisation. As a Project Manager, you may not be able to do much to influence the larger system within which you are working, but it can be helpful to know that there are system dynamics at work, and that there are systems approaches you might be in a position to recommend. We offer three approaches we have found effective for creating an organisational environment that effectively supports spirituality and project management:

1. Alignment: aligning vision, meaning, and purpose at the organisational level.
2. Large systems change: using spiritually-based approaches to integrating change in the entire system, including Open Space Technology and Appreciative Inquiry.
3. Edgewalker Organisational Orientations: understanding, measuring, and aligning the five organisational orientations.

While we provided a basic overview of these methodologies, this book is not designed to be a how-to manual. If any of these approaches are interesting to you, we encourage you to read the related books referenced in the back of this book, and to perhaps consider taking courses or bringing in a certified trainer or facilitator.

The fourth level of spirituality and project management is the planetary level. People, as they develop spiritually, begin to identify and have compassion for more and more of the world outside of themselves, and the field of Project Management parallels that dynamic. As the field of project management has grown and evolved towards Complex Project Management and Program Management, projects are seen as having more impact on interdependent parts of the world. It is up to the awareness of the Project Manager and team members whether this effect is for human benefit or for human harm.

We see convincing evidence that Project Management does more and more good in the world and that the potential is growing. The spiritual models and practices included in this book are powerful tools for helping the enlightened and inspired Project Manager to contribute to humanity and the environment. May all the projects you are a part of be full of meaning and purpose for you, and be a blessing for future generations.

APPENDIX A: INTERNATIONAL FAITH AND SPIRIT AT WORK AWARDS

The International Faith and Spirit at Work Award (formerly the Willis Harman Spirit at Work Award) was created in 2001 to honor companies that have explicit spiritual practices, policies or programs. Forty-seven organisations with a presence in 37 countries have been honoured since 2001.

2002 Honorees

The Body Shop	United Kingdom
Eileen Fisher, Inc.	United States
Embassy Graphics	Canada
Medtronic	United States
Methodist Hospital	United States
Telus Mobility	Canada
Wheaton Franciscan Systems	United States

2003 Honorees

Memorial Hermann Healthcare System	United States
Sounds True, Inc.	United States
SREI International Financial Limited	India
The Times of India	India
Windesheim University of Professional Education	The Netherlands

2004 Honorees

Australia and New Zealand Banking Group Ltd.	Australia, New Zealand
Ascension Health	United States

Centura Health	United States
Excel Industries	India
Hearthstone Homes	United States
PeaceHealth	United States
Phenomenex	USA, UK, Germany, New Zealand and Australia
Planters Development Bank	Philippines
Saint Francis Health Center	United States
Saint Luke's Episcopal Health System	United States

2005 Honorees

Aarti International	India
Catholic Health Initiatives	United States
Central DuPage Hospital	United States
Elcoteq Communications Technology GmbH	Germany
Fachklinik Heiligenfeld GmbH	Germany
Mount Carmel Health	United States
Providence Health Care	Canada
St. Joseph Health Systems	United States
Van Ede and Partners	The Netherlands

2006 Honorees

Clean ServicePower Gmbh	Germany
In Search of Common Ground	United States and Worldwide
Jesuit Social Services	Australia
Nicholas Piramal, Ltd.	India

2007 Honorees

An Cosan	Ireland
Bio-Seehotel Zeulenroda	Germany
Center for Excellence in Leadership	United Kingdom
Conner Partners	United States
Prairie View	United States

Ternary Software	United States
Tyson Foods	United States and Worldwide

2008 Honorees

Berrett-Koehler Publishers	United States
Cordon-Blue Tomasso and Ouimet Tomasso	Canada
Green Mountain Coffee Growers	United States

2011 Honorees

Circle of Life Hospice	United States
University of Winchester	United Kingdom

ABOUT THE INTERNATIONAL FAITH AND SPIRIT AT WORK AWARD

The Award was inspired by the late visionary futurist Willis Harman, PhD (1919–1997).

Selection Criteria

To be selected for an award an organisation must meet the following criteria:

- have at least 20 full-time employees and be at least five years old;

- show that both vertical and horizontal dimensions of Spirituality are demonstrated at the organisation;

- have sustained the explicitly spiritual project, policy or practice being acknowledged for at least one year;

- have a long-term commitment to continuing Spirit at Work initiatives;

- be considered exemplary in its commitment to Spirit at Work.

More information about the awards can be found on the Tyson Center for Faith and Spirituality in the Workplace website (see http://tfsw. uark.edu).

APPENDIX B: QUESTIONS FOR DISCERNMENT AND DISCUSSION WITHIN EACH STAGE OF SPIRAL DYNAMICS

BY SUSIE LEONARD WELLER[1]

Spiral Dynamic Stage	Possible Discernment & Discussion Questions
1. Beige	• Live with Balance and Moderation • How well am I respecting my basic needs? • What are the warning signals that remind me to create more balance? • What helps me to avoid substance abuse or other addictions? • How do I regularly make time for rest, reflection and re-creation?
2. Purple	• Risk Exploring Mystery • How do I deepen my connection to the Divine Mystery? • What choices support personal and spiritual growth? • Do my actions promote faith or fear? • Am I rooted within sacred traditions? Have I become root-bound or rootless like a tumble weed?
3. Red	• Use Power Appropriately • Am I standing in my own power, or trying to please another? • Are my choices empowering or draining energy? • Do my actions respectfully express my thoughts and feelings? • Am I using my power to advocate for those who are vulnerable?

---

1   Used with permission. See www.susieweller.com

4. Blue	• Live by Moral Principles • Does my life have meaning and purpose? • Do my choices increase respect or cause judgment? • How well do I walk my talk? • Am I willing to forgive – myself and others?
5. Orange	• Seek Well-Being for All • Am I expressing my natural gifts and passions, or only the competencies I've developed? • How generously do I share my talents, treasures and time with others? • Do I use science and technology wisely? • Am I willing to express gratitude in all things – even when life is challenging?
6. Green	• Appreciate Unity in Diversity • What helps me to develop inner peace? • In what ways do I collaborate to promote mutual well-being and accountability? • What am I doing to protect the environment? • How does my world view encourage interdependence?
7. Yellow	• Integrate a Holistic Wisdom • How well do I discern among new possibilities to make wise choices? • Am I willing to accept paradoxes and learn from all situations? • What integrates my relationship to the Divine, others, and the planet? • How do I encourage global harmony?
8. Turquoise	• Surrender to Love to Embrace All • Will I let go of my ego to become a clear channel for God's grace? • What helps me become more transparent? • How do I express compassion for everyone? • What restores union with all creation and the Source of Love?
9. Coral	?

REFERENCES

Aburdene, Patricia. 2005. *Megatrends 2010: The Rise of Conscious Capitalism*. Charlottsville, VA: Hampton Roads Publishing.

Aronson, Z.H., Shenhar, A.J. and Reilly, R.R. 2010. Project Spirit: Placing Partaker's Emotions, Attitudes and Norms in the Context of Project Vision, Artifacts, Leader Values, Contextual Performance and Success. *Journal of High Technology Management Research*, 21, 2–13.

Barrett, Richard. 2006. *Building a Values-Driven Organisation: A Whole System Approach to Cultural Transformation*. Cambridge, MA: Butterworth-Heinemann.

Beck, Don and Cowan, Christopher. 1996. *Spiral Dynamics: Mastering Values, Leadership, and Change*. Malden, MA: Blackwell Publishing.

Belbin, R. Meredith. 2010. *Team Roles at Work* (2nd edn). Oxford, UK: Butterworth-Heinemann.

Bennis, Warren. 1999. Foreword, in Mitroff, I. and Denton, E. *A Spiritual Audit of Corporate America: Multiple Designs for Fostering Spirituality in the Workplace*. San Francisco, CA: Jossey-Bass.

Blumenfeld, Laura. 2008. The Shaman of Wall Street. *Washington Post Magazine*, December 7, 9+.

Bohm, David, Nichol, Lee and Senge, Peter. 2004. *On Dialogue*. London, UK: Routledge.

Bolman, Lee and Deal, Terrence. 1995. *Leading with Soul: An Uncommon Journey of Spirit*. San Francisco, CA: Jossey-Bass.

Bowden, Adrian, Lane, Malcom and Martin, Julia. 2001. *Triple Bottom Line Risk Management: Enhancing Profit, Environmental Performance, and Community Benefits*. Hoboken, NJ: Wiley.

Bridges, William and Bridges, Susan. 2009. *Managing Transitions: Making the Most of Change.* Cambridge, MA: De Capo Lifelong Books.

Briskin, Alan, Erickson, Sheryl, Ott, John, and Callanan, Tom. 2009. *The Power of Collective Wisdom and the Trap of Collective Folly.* San Francisco, CA: Berrett-Koehler.

Brittain, Jack. 1998. "Do we Really Mean It?" In Sue Annis Hammond and Cathy Royal (eds), *Lessons from the Field: Applying Appreciative Inquiry.* Plano, TX: Practical Press, 229.

Cleden, David. 2009. *Managing Project Uncertainty.* Farnham, UK: Gower Publishing.

College of Complex Project Managers, and Defence Materiel Organisation. 2006. *Competency Standard for Complex Project Managers.* Canberra: Australian Defence Materiel Organisation.

Conner, Daryl. 1993. *Managing at the Speed of Change: How Resilient Managers Succeed and Prosper Where Others Fail.* New York, NY: Random House.

Cook-Greuter, Susanne. 1990. Maps for Living: Ego-development Stages from Symbiosis to Conscious Universal Embeddedness. In M.L. Commons, C. Armon, L. Kohlberg, F.A. Richards, T.A. Grotzer, and J.D. Sinnott (eds), *Adult Development Vol. 2, Models and Methods in the Study of Adolescent and Adult Thought.* New York, NY: Praeger, 79–104.

Cook-Greuter, Susanne. 1999. *Postautonomous Ego Development: Its Nature and Measurement.* Doctoral dissertation. Cambridge, MA: Harvard Graduate School of Education.

Cooperrider, David and Whitney, Diana. 2005. *Appreciative Inquiry: A Positive Revolution in Change.* San Francisco, CA: Berrett-Koehler.

De Waal, Esther. 1992. *A Seven Day Journey with Thomas Merton.* Polmont, UK: Eagle.

Dombkins, David. 2007. *Complex Project Management: Seminal Essays by Dr David H. Dombkins.* Charleston, SC: BookSurge Publishing.

Fairholm, Gilbert. 1997. *Capturing the Heart of Leadership: Spirituality and Community in the New American Workplace.* Westport, CT: Praeger.

Fowler, James W. 1981. *Stages of Faith.* New York, NY: Harper & Row.

Fox, Matthew. 1994. *The Reinvention of Work: A New Vision of Livelihood for our Time*. San Francisco, CA: HarperCollins.

Fry, Louis W. 2003. Toward a Theory of Spiritual Leadership. *Leadership Quarterly*, 14, 693–727.

Fry, Louis W. 2005. Toward a Theory of Ethical and Spiritual Well-being and Corporate Social Responsibility Through Spiritual Leadership. In Robert A. Giacalone, Carole L. Jurkiewicz and Craig Dunn (eds), *Positive Psychology in Business Ethics and Corporate Responsibility*. Greenwich, CT: Information Age Publishing, 47–83.

Fry, Louis W. 2012. *Maximizing the Triple Bottom Line*. Stanford, CA: Stanford University Press.

Gawain, Shakti. 2002. *Creative Visualization: Using the Power of Your Imagination to Create What You Want in Your Life*. Novato, CA: New World Library.

Gibb, Jack. 1978. *Trust: A New View of Personal and Organisational Development*. Los Angeles, CA: Guild of Tutors Press.

Goleman, Daniel. 1994. *Emotional Intelligence: Why it Can Matter More Than IQ*. New York: Bantam Books.

Gore, Al. 2006. *An Inconvenient Truth*. Documentary produced by Davis Guggenheim.

Greenleaf, Robert K. 1977. *Servant Leadership: A Journey into the Nature of Legitimate Power and Greatness*. Mahwah, NJ: Paulist Press.

Hammond, Sue. 1998. *The Thin Book of Appreciative Inquiry*. Plano, TX: Thin Book Publishing Co.

Handy, Charles. 1994. *The Age of Paradox*. Boston, MA: Harvard Business School Press.

Harpham, Alan and Kippenberger, Tony. 2006. Inspirational Leadership for PPM. Paper at the IPMA World Congress, Shanghai Conference, 2006.

Harrington, James, Conner, Daryl R. and Horney, Nicholas L. 2000. *Project Change Management: Applying Change Management to Improvement Projects*. New York, NY: McGraw-Hill.

Hawken, Paul. 2010. *The Ecology of Commerce Revised Edition: A Declaration of Sustainability*. New York: Harper Books.

Heermann, Barry. 1997. *Building Team Spirit: Activities for Inspiring and Energizing Teams*. New York, NY: McGraw-Hill.

Heermann, Barry. 2004. *Noble Purpose: Igniting Extraordinary Passion for Life and Work*, Fairfax, VA: QSU Publishing.

Hesse, Herman. 1932. *Journey to the East*. Frankfurt am Main: Samuel Fischer.

Hicks, Douglas. 2003. *Religion and the Workplace*. Cambridge, UK: Cambridge University Press.

Hillson, David. 2009. *Managing Risk in Projects*. Farnham, UK: Gower Publishing Ltd.

Howard, Sue and Welbourne, David. 2004. *The Spirit at Work Phenomenon*. London, UK: Azure.

Jaworski, Joseph. 1997. *Synchronicity: The Inner Path of Leadership*. San Francisco, CA: Berrett-Koehler.

Kandarian, Fay. 2003. Personal communication.

Katzenback, Jon and Smith, Douglas. 2003. *The Wisdom of Teams: Creating the High Performance Organization*. New York: Collins Business Essentials.

Kegan, Robert. 1982. *The Evolving Self*. Cambridge, MA: Harvard University Press.

Kegan, Robert. 1994. *In Over our Heads: The Mental Demands of Modern Life*. Cambridge, MA: Harvard University Press.

Keating, Thomas. 2005. *One, The Project*. Feature film. See www.onetheproject.com

I Kings 3: 11–13

Kippenberger, Tony. 2002. *Leadership Express*. Mankato, MN: Capstone.

Kohlberg, Lawrence. 1981. *Essays on Moral Development, Vol. I: The Philosophy of Moral Development*. San Francisco, CA: Harper & Row.

Lamont, Georgeanne. 2002. *The Spirited Business: Success Stories of Soul-Friendly Companies*. London, UK: Hodder & Stoughton.

Levin, Michal. 2001. *Spiritual Intelligence*. London, UK: Coronet.

Loevinger, Jane. 1976. *Ego Development*. San Francisco, CA: Jossey-Bass.

Maddix, Tom. 2005. Providence Health Care Case Study. Unpublished.

Malloch, Theodore Roosevelt. 2008. *Spiritual Enterprise: Doing Virtuous Business*. New York, NY: Encounter Books.

Manz, Charles, Manz, Karen, Marx, Robert and Neck, Christopher. 2001. *The Wisdom of Solomon at Work: Ancient Virtues for Living and Leading Today*. San Francisco, CA: Berrett-Koehler.

Marcic, Dorothy. 1997. *Managing with the Wisdom of Love: Uncovering Virtue in People and Organizations*. San Francisco, CA: Berrett-Koehler.

Maslow, Abraham. 1943. A Theory of Human Motivation. *Psychological Review*, 50(4), 370–96.

Matthew 18:20. 2009. New International Version. Grand Rapids, MI: Zondervan.

McLuhan, T.C. (ed.) 1992. *Touch the Earth: A Self Portrait of Indian Existence*. Edison, NJ: BBS Publishing Corporation.

Merriam-Webster online. Retrieved from http://www.merriam-webster.com/ [accessed August 30, 2010].

Miller, Jill. 2011. *Shaping the Future*. London, UK: Chartered Management Institute.

Mitroff, Ian and Denton, Elizabeth. 1999. *A Spiritual Audit of Corporate America: Multiple Designs for Fostering Spirituality in the Workplace*. San Francisco, CA: Jossey-Bass.

Neal, Judi. 2006. *Edgewalkers: People and Organisations that Take Risks, Build Bridges, and Break New Ground*. Westport, CT: Praeger.

Neal, Judi and Miguez, Joe. 2000. *The Labyrinth: A Life-Giving Tool for Organisations*. Eastern Academy of Management, Philadelphia, PA: May.

Neal, Judi and Hoopes, Linda. 2011. *Assessing Qualities and Skills of Edgewalkers*. Paper submitted to the Academy of Management, Boston, Massachusetts.

Ott, Robert, Kelly, Colleen and Hotchkiss, Marlow. 1997. *LAKES: A Journey of Heroes*. Webster, NY: Xerox Corporation and Living Systems.

Owen, Harrison. 1997. *Open Space Technology: A User's Guide* (2nd edn). San Francisco, CA: Berrett-Koehler.

Owen, Harrison. 1997. *Expanding our Now: The Story of Open Space Technology*. San Francisco, CA: Berrett-Koehler.

Pettifer, Bryan. MODEM. 2002. The Hope of the Managers. Retrieved from www.modem-uk.org/resources/Hope+of+the+Managers.pdf [accessed April 1, 2012].

Piaget, Jean. 1932. *The Moral Judgment of the Child*. London, UK: Kegan Paul, Trench, Trubner & Co.

Pitagorsky, George. 2007. *The Zen Approach to Project Management: Working from Your Center for Balance, Expectations and Performance*. New York, NY: International Institute for Learning.

Porter, Kaye. *Spiral Dynamics*. Retrieved from www.blog.kayeporter.net/tools/spiral-dynamics/ [accessed July 18, 2010].

Rooke, David and Torbert, William. 1999. The CEO's Role in Organizational Transformation. *Systems Thinker*, 10(7), 1–5.

Schweitzer, Albert. 1958. *Peace or Atomic War?* New York, NY: Henry Holt and Company.

Secretan, Lance. 1999. *Inspirational Leadership: Destiny, Calling and Cause*. Toronto: Macmillan.

Secretan, Lance. 2006. *ONE: The Art and Practice of Conscious Leadership*. Ontario: The Secretan Center.

Sense, Andrew and Fernando, Mario. 2011. The Spiritual Identity of Projects. *International Journal of Project Management*, 29(8), 504–13.

Shenhar, A.J., Aronson, Z.H. and Reilly, R.R. 2007. Project Spirit and its Impact on Project Success. In R.R. Reilly (ed.) *The Human Side of Project Management*. Newton Square, PA: Project Management Institute, Inc.

Spears, Larry. (ed.) 1998. *The Power of Servant-Leadership*. San Francisco, CA: Jossey-Bass.

Spence, Kirsty. 2006. Excellence in Sport Management Education: Realizing Human Potential Among Internship Students. Presentation at the Organisational Behavior Teaching Conference, Rochester, NY.

Stephen, Michael. 2002. *Spirituality in Business: The Hidden Success Factor*. Scottsdale, AZ: Inspired Productions Press.

Stone, Daniel. 2009. One Nation under God? Article dated April 7, 2009. Retrieved from www.newsweek.com/2009/04/06/one-nation-under-god.html [accessed June 6, 2010].

Taleb, Nassim Nicholas. 2010. *The Black Swan: The Impact of the Highly Improbable*. New York, NY: Random House Trade Paperbacks.

Toffler, Alvin. 1970. *Future Shock*. New York, NY: Random House.

Tuckman, Bruce. 1977. Developmental Sequence in Small Groups. *Psychological Bulletin*, 63(6), 384–99. Recovered from http://

findarticles.com/p/articles/mi_qa3954/is_200104/ai_n8943663 [accessed November 10, 2008]. Reprinted with permission in Group Facilitation, Spring 2001.

Weller, Susie. Questions for Discernment and Discussion within Each Stage of Spiral Dynamics. Used with permission. See www.susieweller.com

Wheatley, M. 2005. Foreword. In Brown, J., Isaacs, D. and the World Café Community, *The World Cafe: Shaping Our Futures Through Conversations That Matter*. San Francisco, CA: Berrett-Koehler.

Wheeler, M.L. 1996. Diversity: Making the Business Case. December 9, *Business Week*, 89–131.

Whiteley, Richard. 2002. *The Corporate Shaman: A Business Fable*. New York, NY: Harper-Collins.

Wigglesworth, Cindy. 2006. Why Spiritual Intelligence is essential to Mature Leadership. Recovered from http://www.deepchange.com/system/docs/8/original/Spiritual-Intelligence-n-Mature-Leadership.pdf?1311106089 [accessed March 31, 2012].

Wigglesworth, Cindy. 2010. Spiritual Intelligence: Why it Matters. Recovered from www.consciouspursuits.com/Articles/SIWhyIt Matters.pdf [accessed July 19, 2010].

Wilber, Ken. 2001. A Theory of Everything: An Integral Vision for Business, Politics. *Science and Spirituality*. Boston, MA: Shambhala Press.

Wilkinson, Richard and Pickett, Kate. 2011. *The Spirit Level: Why Greater Equality Makes Societies Stronger*. London, UK: Bloomsbury Press.

Wright, Clive. 2005. *The Business of Virtue*. Kelowna, BC: Wood Lake Books.

Zohar, Danah and Marshall, Ian. 2000. *SQ: Connecting with our Spiritual Intelligence*. London, UK: Bloomsbury.

INDEX

Locators shown in *italics* refer to tables and figures.

ADVANCES IN PROJECT MANAGEMENT

Advances in Project Management provides short, state of play guides to the main aspects of the new emerging applications, including: maturity models, agile projects, extreme projects, Six Sigma and projects, human factors and leadership in projects, project governance, value management, virtual teams and project benefits.

CURRENTLY PUBLISHED TITLES

REVIEWS OF THE SERIES

Managing Project Uncertainty, David Cleden

> *This is a must-read book for anyone involved in project management. The author's carefully crafted work meets all my "4Cs" review criteria. The book is clear, cogent, concise and complete ... it is a brave author who essays to write about managing project uncertainty in a text extending to only 117 pages (soft-cover version). In my opinion, David Cleden succeeds brilliantly. ... For project managers this book, far from being a short-lived stress anodyne, will provide a confidence-boosting tonic. Project uncertainty? Bring it on, I say!*
>
> International Journal of Managing Projects in Business

> *Uncertainty is an inevitable aspect of most projects, but even the most proficient project manager struggles to successfully contain it. Many projects overrun and consume more funds than were originally budgeted, often leading to unplanned expense and outright programme failure. David examines how uncertainty occurs and provides management strategies that the user can put to immediate use on their own project work. He also provides a series of pre-emptive uncertainty and risk avoidance strategies that should be the cornerstone of any planning exercise for all personnel involved in project work.*
>
> *I have been delivering both large and small projects and programmes in the public and private sector since 1989. I wish this book had been available when I began my career in project work. I strongly commend this book to all project professionals.*
>
> Lee Hendricks, Sales & Marketing Director,
> SunGard Public Sector

> *The book under review is an excellent presentation of a comprehensive set of explorations about uncertainty (its recognition) in the context of projects. It does a good job of all along reinforcing the difference between risk (known unknowns) management and managing uncertainty (unknown unknowns –*

"bolt from the blue"). The author lucidly presents a variety of frameworks/models so that the reader easily grasps the varied forms in which uncertainty presents itself in the context of projects.

VISION: The Journal of Business Perspective (India)

Cleden will leave you with a sound understanding about the traits, tendencies, timing and tenacity of uncertainty in projects. He is also adept at identifying certain methods that try to contain the uncertainty, and why some prove more successful than others. Those who expect risk management to be the be-all, end-all for uncertainty solutions will be in for a rude awakening.

Brad Egeland, Project Management Tips

Strategic Project Risk Appraisal and Management, Elaine Harris

Elaine Harris's volume is timely. In a world of books by "instant experts" it's pleasing to read something by someone who clearly knows their onions, and has a passion for the subject. In summary, this is a thorough and engaging book.

Chris Morgan, Head of Business Assurance
for Select Plant Hire, Quality World

As soon as I met Elaine I realised that we both shared a passion to better understand the inherent risk in any project, be that capital investment, expansion capital or expansion of assets. What is seldom analysed are the components of knowledge necessary to make a good judgement, the impact of our own prejudices in relation to projects or for that matter the cultural elements within an organisation which impact upon the decision making process. Elaine created a system to break this down and give reasons and logic to both the process and the human interaction necessary to improve the chances of success. Adopting her recommendations will improve teamwork and outcomes for your company.

Edward Roderick Hon. LLD, former CEO Christian Salvesen plc

Project-Oriented Leadership, Ralf Müller and J Rodney Turner

> *Müller and Turner have compiled a terrific "ready-reckoner" that all project managers would benefit from reading and reflecting upon to challenge their performance. The authors have condensed considerable experience and research from a wide variety of professional disciplines, to provide a robust digest that highlights the significance of leadership capabilities for effective delivery of project outcomes. One of the big advantages of this book is the richness of the content and the natural flow of their argument throughout such a short book....Good advice, well explained and backed up with a body of evidence...I will be recommending the book to colleagues who are in project leader and manager roles and to students who are considering these as part of their development or career path.'*
>
> Arthur Shelley, RMIT University, Melbourne, Australia,
> *International Journal of Managing Projects in Business*

> *In a remarkably succinct 89 pages, Müller and Turner review an astonishing depth of evidence, supported by their own (published) research which challenges many of the commonly held assumptions not only about project management, but about what makes for successful leaders.*
>
> *This book is clearly written more for the project-manager type personality than for the natural leader. Concision, evidence and analysis are the main characteristics of the writing style...it is massively authoritative, and so carefully written that a couple of hours spent in its 89 pages may pay huge dividends compared to the more expansive, easy reading style of other management books.*
>
> Mike Turner, Director of Communications for NHS
> Warwickshire

Tame, Messy and Wicked Risk Leadership, David Hancock

> *This book takes project risk management firmly onto a higher and wider plane. We thought we knew what project risk management*

was and what it could do. David Hancock shows us a great deal more of both. David Hancock has probably read more about risk management than almost anybody else; he has almost certainly thought about it as much as anybody else and he has quite certainly learnt from doing it on very difficult projects as much as anybody else. His book draws fully on all three components. For a book which tackles a complex subject with breadth, insight and novelty – it's remarkable that it is also a really good read. I could go on!

Dr Martin Barnes CBE FREng, President, The Association for Project Management

This compact and thought-provoking description of risk management will be useful to anybody with responsibilities for projects, programmes or businesses. It hits the nail on the head in so many ways, for example by pointing out that risk management can easily drift into a checklist mindset, driven by the production of registers of numerous occurrences characterised by the Risk = Probablity × Consequence equation. David Hancock points out that real life is much more complicated, with the heart of the problem lying in people, so that real life resembles poker rather than roulette. He also points out that while the important thing is to solve the right problem, many real-life issues cannot be readily described in a definitive statement of the problem. There are often interrelated individual problems with surrounding social issues and he describes these real-life situations as "Wicked Messes". Unusual terminology, but definitely worth the read, as much for the overall problem description as for the recommended strategies for getting to grips with real-life risk management. I have no hesitation in recommending this *book.*

Sir Robert Walmsley KCB FREng, Chairman of the Board of the Major Projects Association

In highlighting the complexity of many of today's problems and defining them as tame, messy or wicked, David Hancock brings a new perspective to the risk issues that we currently face. He challenges risk managers, and particularly those involved in

*project risk management, to take a much broader approach
to the assessment of risk and consider the social, political and
behavioural dimensions of each problem, as well as the scientific
and engineering aspects with which they are most comfortable.
In this way, risks will be viewed more holistically and managed
more effectively than at present.*

Dr Lynn T. Drennan, Chief Executive Alarm,
The Public Risk Management Association

ABOUT THE EDITOR

Professor Darren Dalcher is founder and Director of the National Centre
for Project Management, a Professor of Software Project Management at
Middlesex University and Visiting Professor of Computer Science at the
University of Iceland. Professor Dalcher has been named by the Association
for Project Management as one of the top 10 'movers and shapers' in project
management. He has also been voted *Project Magazine*'s Academic of the
Year for his contribution in 'integrating and weaving academic work with
practice'.

Professor Dalcher is active in numerous international committees, steering
groups and editorial boards. He is heavily involved in organising international
conferences, and has delivered many keynote addresses and tutorials. He
has written over 150 papers and book chapters on project management and
software engineering. He is Editor-in-Chief of *Software Process Improvement
and Practice*, an international journal focusing on capability, maturity, growth
and improvement.

Professor Dalcher is a Fellow of the Association for Project Management and the
British Computer Society, and a Member of the Project Management Institute, the
Academy of Management, the Institute for Electrical and Electronics Engineers
and the Association for Computing Machinery. He is a Chartered IT Practitioner.
He is a member of the PMI Advisory Board responsible for the prestigious David I.
Cleland project management award, and of the APM Professional Development
Board.

National Centre for Project Management
Middlesex University
College House
Trent Park
Bramley Road
London N14 4YZ
Email: ncpm@mdx.ac.uk
Phone: +44 (0)20 8411 2299